Brown v. Board of Education

by James Tackach

FAMOUS TRIALS

Lucent Books, San Diego, CA

Other books in the Famous Trials series:

The Boston Massacre   The Salem Witch Trials
The Dred Scott Decision   The Scopes Trial
The Nuremberg Trials   The Trial of Joan of Arc
The O.J. Simpson Trial   The Trial of Socrates

Library of Congress Cataloging-in-Publication Data

Tackach, James.
  Brown v. Board of Education / by James Tackach.
    p. cm. — (Famous trials)
  Includes bibliographical references and index.
  Summary: Provides a historical overview of the case that desegregated public education in the United States.
  ISBN 1-56006-273-8 (alk. paper)
  1. Brown, Oliver, 1918– —Trials, litigation, etc.—Juvenile literature. 2. Topeka (Kans.). Board of Education—Trials, litigation, etc.—Juvenile literature. 3. Segregation in education—Law and legislation—United States—Juvenile literature. [1. Brown, Oliver, 1918– —Trials, litigation, etc. 2. Segregation in education—Law and legislation. 3. Afro-Americans—Civil rights.] I. Title. II. Series: Famous trials series.
KF228.B76T33   1998
344.73'0798—dc21   97-7482
                                                      CIP
                                                       AC

Table of Contents

Foreword

"The law is not an end in and of itself, nor does it provide ends. It is preeminently a means to serve what we think is right."

William J. Brennan Jr.

THE CONCEPT OF JUSTICE AND THE RULE OF LAW are hallmarks of Western civilization, manifested perhaps most visibly in widely famous and dramatic court trials. These trials include such important and memorable personages as the ancient Greek philosopher Socrates, who was accused and convicted of corrupting the minds of his society's youth in 399 B.C.; the French maiden and military leader Joan of Arc, accused and convicted of heresy against the church in 1431; to former football star O.J. Simpson, acquitted of double murder in 1995. These and other well-known and controversial trials constitute the most public, and therefore most familiar, demonstrations of a Western legal tradition that dates back through the ages. Although no one is certain when the first law code appeared or when the first formal court trials were held, Babylonian ruler Hammurabi introduced the first known law code in about 1760 B.C. It remains unclear how this code was administered, and no records of specific trials have survived. What is clear, however, is that humans have always sought to govern behavior and define actions in terms of law.

Almost all societies have made laws and prosecuted people for going against those laws, but the question of which behaviors to sanction and which to censure has always been controversial and remains in flux. Some, such as Roman orator and legislator Cicero, argue that laws are simply applications of universal standards. Cicero believed that humanity would agree on what constituted illegal behavior and that human laws were a mere extension of natural laws. "True law is right reason in agreement with nature," he wrote,

4

world-wide in scope, unchanging, everlasting. . . . We may not oppose or alter that law, we cannot abolish it, we cannot be freed from its obligations by any legislature. . . .This [natural] law does not differ for Rome and for Athens, for the present and for the future. . . . It is and will be valid for all nations and all times.

Cicero's rather optimistic view has been contradicted throughout history, however. For every law made to preserve harmony and set universal standards of behavior, another has been born of fear, prejudice, greed, desire for power, and a host of other motives. History is replete with individuals defying and fighting to change such laws—and even to topple governments that dictate such laws. Abolitionists fought against slavery, civil rights leaders fought for equal rights, millions throughout the world have fought for independence—these constitute a minimum of reasons for which people have sought to overturn laws that they believed to be wrong or unjust. In opposition to Cicero, then, many others, such as eighteenth-century English poet and philosopher William Godwin, believe humans must be constantly vigilant against bad laws. As Godwin said in 1793:

Laws we sometimes call the wisdom of our ancestors. But this is a strange imposition. It was as frequently the dictate of their passion, of timidity, jealousy, a monopolizing spirit, and a lust of power that knew no bounds. Are we not obliged perpetually to renew and remodel this misnamed wisdom of our ancestors? To correct it by a detection of their ignorance, and a censure of their intolerance?

Lucent Books' *Famous Trials* series showcases trials that exemplify both society's praiseworthy condemnation of universally unacceptable behavior, and its misguided persecution of individuals based on fear and ignorance, as well as trials that leave open the question of whether justice has been done. Each volume begins by setting the scene and providing a historical context to show how society's mores influence the trial process and the verdict.

Each book goes on to present a detailed and lively account of the trial, including liberal use of primary source material such as direct testimony, lawyers' summations, and contemporary and modern commentary. In addition, sidebars throughout the text create a broader context by presenting illuminating details about important points of law, information on key personalities, and important distinctions related to civil, federal, and criminal procedures. Thus, all of the primary and secondary source material included in both the text and the sidebars demonstrates to readers the sources and methods historians use to derive information and conclusions about such events.

Lastly, each *Famous Trials* volume includes one or more of the following comprehensive tools that motivate readers to pursue further reading and research. A timeline allows readers to see the scope of the trial at a glance, annotated bibliographies provide both sources for further research and a thorough list of works consulted, a glossary helps students with unfamiliar words and concepts, and a comprehensive index permits quick scanning of the book as a whole.

The insight of Oliver Wendell Holmes Jr., distinguished Supreme Court justice, exemplifies the theme of the *Famous Trials* series. Taken from *The Common Law*, published in 1881, Holmes remarked: "The life of the law has not been logic, it has been experience." That "experience" consists mainly in how laws are applied in society and challenged in the courts, a process resulting in differing outcomes from one generation to the next. Thus, the *Famous Trials* series encourages readers to examine trials within a broader historical and social context.

Introduction

A Supreme Court Decision That Changed America

THE SUPREME COURT OF THE UNITED STATES is perhaps the most remarkable legal institution in the entire world. The Court, which is composed of nine middle-aged judges who conduct their business in a large and imposing classical-style building in Washington, D.C., creates no laws, commands no army, and generally remains aloof from the political battles that often occupy the president and members of Congress. Yet through its written opinions, the Supreme Court often changes the course of American history.

The U.S. Constitution charges the Supreme Court with interpreting the laws of the land. Specifically, the Court reviews the decisions of lower courts—state courts, federal courts, and appeals courts—and determines whether those decisions are consistent with the Constitution. If the Supreme Court agrees with the decision of a lower court, that decision is upheld and becomes binding on all parties. If the Supreme Court judges that the finding of a lower court contradicts the Constitution, that finding is overruled and becomes invalid.

Each year the Supreme Court reviews a dozen or more lower-court cases and issues its opinions. Some of these opinions affect only a small number of people, perhaps only the handful of individuals involved in the case that the Court reviewed. On occasion, however, a Supreme Court decision has a far-reaching impact, affecting millions of people around the entire United States and reshaping American politics and culture. That is what happened in May 1954 when the Court delivered its opinion in a case titled *Brown v. Board of Education of Topeka, Kansas.*

The *Brown v. Board of Education* case concerned segregation in the country's public schools. Before 1954 most public school systems in the South—and some in the North as well—were racially segregated. White children attended one school, and black children enrolled in another. In some cities and towns, school segregation was enforced by laws; in other places, the schools were segregated by custom and tradition. In the South, segregation laws—called Jim Crow laws—also separated the races in public parks, theaters, and athletic stadiums. Neighborhoods, hotels, restaurants, railroad cars, and other public accommodations were also rigidly segregated. Although the defenders of Jim Crow policies might state otherwise, the obvious purpose of segregation laws was to keep African Americans—the children and grandchildren of slaves—in an inferior position in American

This photo of a segregated school is testament to the inferior conditions black children were forced to endure prior to the historic decision in Brown v. Board of Education.

society, to prevent them from enjoying the social, political, and economic opportunities widely available to white Americans.

The Supreme Court's decision in the *Brown v. Board of Education* case marked the beginning of the end of racial segregation in the United States. When the Court ruled in 1954 that school segregation laws violated the Fourteenth Amendment of the U.S. Constitution, the Court demolished the legal foundation on which racial segregation stood. The Court's opinion, written and delivered by Chief Justice Earl Warren, also served as a stirring moral indictment of racial segregation, an eloquent challenge to America to cast off its prejudices and extend its promises of life, liberty, and the pursuit of happiness to all citizens, regardless of race or color.

As historian David Halberstam states in his history of the 1950s: "The *Brown v. Board of Education* decision not only legally ended segregation, it deprived segregationist practices of their moral legitimacy as well. It was therefore perhaps the single most important moment of the decade, the moment that separated the old order from the new and helped create the tumultuous era just arriving." When Chief Justice Warren asserted that "in the field of public education" segregation "has no place," he aimed the nation in a bold new direction, a road on which it could never turn back.

Chapter 1

A Nation Divided

ON JUNE 16, 1858, IN THE TOWN of Springfield, Illinois, a prominent member of the newly formed Republican Party delivered an address that became known thereafter as the "House Divided" speech. The speaker, Abraham Lincoln, warned his fellow citizens that their nation's policy on slavery—outlawing forced servitude in the North and protecting it in the South—would eventually cause the country to dissolve. "A house divided against itself cannot stand," said Lincoln. "I believe this government cannot endure permanently *half slave* and *half free*."

The United States had been so divided since its birth. Despite the guarantees asserted in the Declaration of Independence in 1776—"That all men are created equal, that they are endowed by their Creator with certain unalienable Rights, that among these are Life, Liberty and the pursuit of Happiness"—the men who established the American republic at the Philadelphia Convention of 1787 allowed the institution of slavery, begun in the English colonies in 1617, to remain in place. Their Constitution both tolerated and protected slavery; and though the institution would, by 1800, virtually disappear in the North, it persisted and prospered in the South, creating a sharply divided nation comprising a group of free states and a group of slave states. In 1861, less than three years after Lincoln delivered his prophetic words in Springfield, the divided nation did indeed begin to dissolve. For the next four years, President Lincoln would lead the Northern states in a bloody civil war waged in an effort to keep his divided house from falling. Near the end of that war, Lincoln, in his Second Inaugural

Address, expressed his fervent desire to reunite his divided house—"to bind up the nation's wounds" and "to do all which may achieve and cherish a just, and a lasting peace among ourselves, and with nations."

Despite the wishes of President Lincoln, who fell to an assassin's bullet several weeks after delivering his Second Inaugural Address, the United States would remain stubbornly divided for another one hundred years. The Civil War ended American slavery, but the country's racial divisions persisted. A century after the war ended, the federal government of the United States was only beginning to dismantle the legal, political, and social barriers that rigidly divided white and black Americans.

President Abraham Lincoln is remembered for his fierce devotion to the preservation of the Union and for his stand against slavery.

Amending the Constitution

In the aftermath of the Civil War, the governmental leaders of the victorious Northern states saw that merely ending slavery would not alone break down the racial divisions that existed across the entire United States, particularly in the South, where four million African American slaves had been suddenly set free. Hoping to ensure the civil rights of freed slaves, the U.S. Congress initiated the passage of three constitutional amendments and two civil rights acts designed to extend the full benefits of citizenship to the newly freed slaves.

The men who wrote the U.S. Constitution in 1787 wisely allowed for the great document to be amended by succeeding generations. An amendment can be proposed if two-thirds of the members of the Senate and House of Representatives deem the measure necessary. If such a proposal musters the required number of votes in Congress, the measure is sent to the legislatures of the individual states. If three-fourths of the state legislative bodies approve the amendment, it becomes a permanent part of the Constitution. Even before the Constitution was enacted, the document was amended ten times. The first ten amendments to the Constitution—called the Bill of Rights—guaranteed U.S. citizens freedom of religion, freedom of speech, freedom from unwarranted searches and seizure by government officials, a trial by an impartial jury, and other important rights and liberties. The Eleventh Amendment, concerning the judicial powers of the United States, was added in 1798, and the Twelfth Amendment, which adjusted the process of electing the president and vice president, became part of the Constitution in 1804. No new amendments were enacted during the next sixty years.

The Civil War Amendments

The Thirteenth Amendment to the Constitution was already under consideration before the Civil War had ended. In 1863 President Lincoln, acting as commander in chief of the armed forces, issued the Emancipation Proclamation, which freed all slaves in the states that had seceded from the United States at the start of the Civil War. Surmising that the president's action might be judged contrary to the Constitution, the political leaders of the North determined to end slavery by enacting a constitutional amendment. The Thirteenth Amendment—which stated that "Neither slavery nor involuntary servitude, except as a punishment for crime . . . shall exist within the United States"—received congressional approval in 1864 and was ratified by the required number of states in December 1865, several months after the Civil War had ended.

Although the Thirteenth Amendment freed all the slaves, it did nothing to guarantee that they would be able to enjoy the rights and privileges of American citizenship. In the South, the freed African Americans were generally despised. During the

Excitement permeates the House of Representatives after the passage of the Thirteenth Amendment. Although the amendment abolished slavery, severe racism prohibited freed slaves from enjoying the full privileges of American citizenship.

Civil War, the Southern states had suffered greatly. Cities, towns, and individual farms and homes had been ruined, and the South's economy was in shambles. Many citizens of the defeated Confederate states blamed the freed slaves for this devastating situation. Many Southerners believed that the ex-slaves had to be punished. Freed slaves would not be allowed to vote or own property. Black children would not be able to enroll in schools. Many communities in the South enacted what became known as the Black Codes, a series of laws designed to restrict the freedom of the new freemen. An ex-slave who had been deported from his old plantation could be arrested for vagrancy and forced to work for any landowner who paid his fine. Freed slaves were compelled to purchase expensive licenses simply to be eligible to apply for a job. Freed blacks who committed even minor crimes were issued excessively stiff penalties. And resentment of the African American was not restricted to the South. Freed blacks who moved to the North in search of better opportunity would compete against whites for jobs, and many white Northerners, as a result, resented the newcomers.

These conditions led Congress to pass the Civil Rights Act of 1866. The bill gave all citizens, regardless of race, the right to make and enforce contracts, the right to own and sell property, and the right to file lawsuits in court when these and other personal rights were denied. The new law also contained language that guaranteed the "full and equal benefit of all laws and proceedings" to all American citizens. President Andrew Johnson, who took office after President Lincoln's death, initially vetoed the bill, but Congress overrode the president's veto with a two-thirds majority vote. This majority was achieved mainly because the congressional delegations of the Southern states that had seceded from the Union at the start of the Civil War had not yet been readmitted to Congress.

After the passage of the Civil Rights Act of 1866, however, some members of Congress feared that the Supreme Court might deem the new law unconstitutional on some grounds. These concerns led to the proposal and eventual enactment of another constitutional amendment. In June 1866 Congress proposed the

Groups of citizens celebrate the passage of the Civil Rights Act of 1866. While the act did not completely eradicate racism, it laid the groundwork for the Fourteenth and Fifteenth Amendments.

Fourteenth Amendment to the Constitution. The proposal's main purpose was simple: to extend the rights and privileges of citizenship to all Americans, regardless of race or ancestry. The amendment asserted that all persons born in the United States would be classified as citizens; and as citizens, these individuals would enjoy the full protection of the law. The individual states were prohibited from passing any law that would restrict the rights and privileges of American citizens. Nor could any state "deny to any person within its jurisdiction the equal protection of the laws." The amendment gave Congress the power "to enforce, by appropriate legislation, the provisions of this article."

The Fourteenth Amendment had little chance of passing; it would not be approved by the required three-fourths of the state legislatures because the entire South opposed it. Indeed, the legislative bodies of ten of the eleven states of the old Confederacy voted down the measure. The Northern Republicans who controlled Congress after the Civil War decided to force the Southern states to approve the new amendment. In March 1866 Congress passed the first Reconstruction Act, which disbanded the legislatures of the ten states that refused to ratify the Fourteenth Amendment. These states were ordered to write new state constitutions and to approve the Fourteenth Amendment; if they did not, their congressional delegations would be unseated. Eventually, the recalcitrant Southern states complied, and the Fourteenth Amendment became a permanent part of the Constitution in 1868.

Voting and Public Facilities

The following year Congress again acted on behalf of the freed African American slaves. In February 1869 Congress proposed the Fifteenth Amendment to the Constitution. The amendment contains two sections, each just one sentence long. Section 1 states: "The rights of citizens of the United States to vote shall not be denied or abridged by the United States or by any State on account of race, color, or previous condition of servitude." Section 2 states: "The Congress shall have power to enforce this article by appropriate legislation." The Fifteenth Amendment

THE EQUAL PROTECTION CLAUSE

The key component of the Fourteenth Amendment to the Constitution is Section 1, which contains the "equal protection" clause. That clause, designed to protect the rights of black citizens after the Civil War, asserts that all American citizens are equal under the law. The equal protection clause became the basis for the Supreme Court's decision in *Brown v. Board of Education* and for the wave of civil rights legislation that followed it.

> All persons born or naturalized in the United States and subject to the jurisdiction thereof, are citizens of the United States and of the State wherein they reside. No State shall make or enforce any law which shall abridge the privileges or immunities of citizens of the United States; nor shall any State deprive any person of life, liberty, or property, without due process of law; nor deny to any person within its jurisdiction the equal protection of the laws.

attempted to block the concerted effort by many Southern states to keep black citizens from the ballot box. Thirteen months later the amendment was passed by the required number of state legislatures, and it became a permanent part of the Constitution.

In 1875, acting under its mandate to pass appropriate legislation to support the provisions of the Fourteenth Amendment, Congress proposed another piece of civil rights legislation designed to curtail racial segregation. The Civil Rights Act of 1875 attempted to grant to all American citizens, regardless of race or color, "the full and equal enjoyment of the accommodations . . . of inns, public conveyances on land or water, theatres and other places of public enjoyment." The bill also contained a provision that outlawed the practice of disallowing black citizens from serving on courtroom juries. Senator Charles Sumner of Massachusetts argued for the inclusion of another provision in this bill—language that would outlaw segregation in public schools—but his attempt was not successful.

Hence, during the decade after the Civil War, the Congress of the United States made a serious effort to raze the barriers that separated black and white citizens. On paper, the effort to unite the divided house that Lincoln had spoken about in 1858 was certainly underway. In reality, black Americans would not begin to enjoy the rights and freedoms guaranteed by the Thirteenth, Fourteenth, and Fifteenth Amendments and by the Civil Rights Acts of 1866 and 1875 for almost another century.

The Jim Crow Era

Lawmakers and citizens throughout the South acted swiftly to block the federal government's effort to extend to African Americans the full rights and privileges of citizenship. In 1866 an ex-Confederate general, Nathan Bedford Forrest of Tennessee, established the Ku Klux Klan. The Klan, founded at first as a political organization, spread throughout the South, soon becoming a terrorist paramilitary force whose main function was to intimidate black citizens who attempted to register to vote or demanded other civil rights. Disguised in white hoods and gowns, Klansmen conducted their business by burning black

This image of Ku Klux Klan members appeared in an 1868 Harper's Weekly. *Their violent tactics struck terror in the hearts of newly freed blacks.*

people's homes, beating black citizens, and even murdering blacks and whites who helped and sympathized with them.

Though many citizens throughout the South condemned the violent and illegal actions of the Klan, the region's lawmakers supported the organization's goals. Throughout the South, state legislatures passed laws designed to deny the civil and political rights of African Americans. To prevent black citizens from voting, a stiff voting fee—called a "poll tax"—was imposed in many areas of the South. Statutes known as "grandfather clauses" also became widespread throughout the South. These laws stipulated that a person could not register to vote if any of his four grandparents had been a slave. Bills were passed by Southern legislatures to prevent blacks from serving on juries.

Southern lawmakers also acted to deny the social rights and privileges of black citizens. Towns and cities passed laws that prevented blacks from lodging in certain hotels, eating in certain restaurants, and traveling in the same train cars as whites. African Americans were prohibited from applying to all but the most menial jobs, and black workers who were able to find employment were paid much less than whites performing the same tasks. Doctors and hospitals refused to minister to black patients, even in life-and-death situations. And black children were prohibited from enrolling in the free public schools that were being established throughout the South in the decades after the Civil War.

The legal measures, which essentially continued the Black Codes that the states of the old Confederacy established after the Civil War, became known as Jim Crow laws, named after a character who frequently appeared in Negro minstrel shows of the nineteenth century. The Jim Crow era would continue in the South until the middle of the twentieth century.

By passing Jim Crow laws, Southern legislatures were certainly violating the spirit of the constitutional amendments and accompanying civil rights laws passed after the Civil War. In the United States, the task of determining whether a law violates the Constitution belongs to the judicial branch of the government— the state and federal court system. Any citizen or group of citizens is entitled to file a lawsuit to determine whether a local,

JUDICIAL REVIEW

In the United States, the Constitution is the supreme law of the land. Any law passed by Congress, by a state legislature, or by a town or city council must not violate the articles and amendments of the Constitution. The task of interpreting the laws, of deciding whether a law contradicts the Constitution, belongs to the judicial branch of government, the state and federal court system. The final arbiter in determining if a law is constitutional is the U.S. Supreme Court.

Chief Justice John Marshall established the principle of judicial review in the 1803 case Marbury v. Madison.

A typical case that reaches the Supreme Court will have been heard by at least one or two lower courts. For example, a citizen who files a lawsuit to test the constitutionality of a law in California would bring his suit to the California Supreme Court. If the California court ruled against the person who initiated the lawsuit (called the plaintiff), the plaintiff can appeal the case in a federal court of appeals, which can uphold or overturn the state court's ruling. Either party can appeal the decision of the appeals court to the Supreme Court. The Supreme Court, if it decides to hear the case, could uphold or overturn the appeals court's ruling. The Supreme Court's judgment is final and binding on all parties.

This power to judge whether laws are in agreement with the Constitution is called judicial review. The concept, an American legal innovation, was established by Chief Justice John Marshall in the 1803 case titled *Marbury v. Madison*. In 1801, on his final day as president, John Adams appointed William Marbury as a justice of the peace for the District of Columbia. Adams's secretary of state, President-elect Thomas Jefferson, refused to deliver Marbury's commission, and Marbury asked the Supreme Court to issue an order confirming his appointment. Chief Justice Marshall refused Marbury's request, asserting that the Judiciary Act of 1789, which allowed the Court to issue such orders, contradicted the language of the Constitution. Marshall's statement that "it is emphatically the province and duty of the judicial department to say what the law is" established the principle of judicial review.

state, or federal law squares with the Constitution. A court decides whether the law in question violates the Constitution. A decision by a state or federal court can be appealed to a higher court by any party in the lawsuit. The highest court in the country is the Supreme Court. The Supreme Court's decision is binding on all parties in any lawsuit; there can be no appeal of a Supreme Court decision.

Civil Rights Cases in the 1800s

During the last quarter of the nineteenth century, the Supreme Court reviewed several cases involving civil rights issues, including the landmark case of *Plessy v. Ferguson*. The result was that as the nineteenth century came to an end, Jim Crow legislation was still firmly in place.

In 1875 the Supreme Court reviewed a lower-court ruling in a case titled *United States v. Reese*. William Garner, a black man from Lexington, Kentucky, filed a complaint against election officials because he was turned away at the polls when he attempted to exercise his right to vote. Federal officials, acting under the Fifteenth Amendment, arrested the local officials who had turned away Garner at the polls. The conviction of the local voting officials was appealed to the Supreme Court. Chief Justice Morrison Waite, writing the Court's opinion, stated that the Fifteenth Amendment did not guarantee any citizen the right to vote. It merely prohibited states from denying the vote to any citizen because of his race. Reese had to prove that he was denied the right to vote solely because he was black. According to the Supreme Court, he had not done so.

That same year a Supreme Court decision titled *United States v. Cruikshank* seriously weakened the power of both the Fourteenth and Fifteenth Amendments. This Louisiana case resulted from an incident that occurred at a political rally of black citizens. A group of about one hundred white men had used violence to disrupt the rally, and two of the whites were indicted under laws supporting the Fifteenth Amendment. The Supreme Court overturned the conviction because the original indictment had not specifically charged the two convicted white men with harassing the blacks at the rally because of their race. The Court acknowledged that the black citizens might have had their rights violated, but those violations were caused by private citizens, not by the state. The Court ruled that the Fourteenth Amendment prohibits any state government from violating the rights of citizens, but the amendment does not specifically prohibit a group of citizens from violating the rights of other citizens. Hence, the Supreme Court was reading the Fourteenth and Fifteenth Amendments very narrowly; the Court seemed to be looking for any reason to deny black citizens the rights of citizenship guaranteed by those amendments.

The Supreme Court decision in *United States v. Harris*, in 1883, relied on the precedent set in the *United States v. Cruikshank* decision several years earlier. The *Harris* case concerned an armed mob of white citizens who broke into a jail in Tennessee and severely beat several black men held in custody by a local sheriff. One of the inmates was beaten so badly that he died. When the case reached the Supreme Court on appeal, the Court ruled that the civil rights of the black prisoners had not been violated because the action against them was not taken by state law enforcement officials. The inmates had been beaten by a mob of private citizens, and, the Court reasoned, the Fourteenth Amendment protected citizens only from unlawful actions perpetrated by the state.

Shortly after issuing its opinion in *United States v. Harris*, the Supreme Court ruled on several cases involving the Civil Rights Act of 1875. These cases involved black citizens who had been denied access to hotels, theaters, and other public places—actions specifically outlawed by the Civil Rights Act. In a decision titled *The Civil Rights Cases*, the Court ruled the act unconstitutional, arguing that Congress had overstepped its authority by compelling the owners of private businesses to serve any citizen regardless of race. The Court asserted that the Fourteenth Amendment prohibited only the states—not private businesses—from denying a citizen his or her rights on the basis of race.

These Supreme Court decisions considerably weakened the power of the Fourteenth and Fifteenth Amendments, ensuring that the era of Jim Crow would continue. The Court gave further support for Jim Crow legislation in the landmark case titled *Plessy v. Ferguson*, creating a precedent that would stand until the *Brown v. Board of Education of Topeka, Kansas*, case of 1954.

Homer Plessy's Lawsuit

Plessy v. Ferguson concerned a piece of Jim Crow legislation that had been enacted in Louisiana in 1890. The law, titled the Louisiana Railway Accommodations Act, required all railway companies operating in the state to "provide equal but separate accommodations for the white and colored races, by providing separate coaches or compartments so as to secure separate accommodations." Any passenger "insisting on going into a coach or compartment to which by his race he does not belong, shall be liable to a fine of twenty-five dollars or in lieu thereof to imprisonment for a period of not more than twenty days." On June 7, 1892, Homer Plessy, a man who was seven-eighths white and one-eighth black, but still considered a Negro under Louisiana law, boarded a train in New Orleans and took a seat in the car reserved for white travelers. He was arrested by a detective and taken to the Criminal District Court of New Orleans, where Judge John Ferguson issued the penalty required by law. Citing the Fourteenth Amendment, Plessy appealed his conviction to the Louisiana Supreme Court, which allowed him to appeal to the U.S. Supreme Court.

On May 6, 1896, the Supreme Court issued its opinion in *Plessy v. Ferguson*. By a 7-1 vote the Court upheld Plessy's conviction. Associate Justice Henry Billings Brown, delivering the Court's decision, granted that the object of the Fourteenth Amendment was "undoubtedly to enforce the absolute equality of the two races before the law," but the amendment "could not have been intended to abolish distinctions based on color." He added that laws separating the races "do not necessarily imply the inferiority of either race to the other." Brown granted that all laws should be enacted "for the promotion for the public good, and not for the annoyance or oppression of a particular class," yet he maintained that a law requiring the separation of races on a public railway is no "more obnoxious to the Fourteenth Amendment than the acts of Congress requiring separate schools for colored children in the District of Columbia." Justice Brown

PLESSY V. FERGUSON:
JUSTICE HARLAN'S DISSENT

Only one Supreme Court justice dissented from the majority opinion in *Plessy v. Ferguson:* Justice John Marshall Harlan of Kentucky, a former slave owner who had joined the Union Army during the Civil War. Justice Harlan's written dissenting opinion provided a stirring defense of the spirit of the Fourteenth Amendment and asserted an interpretation of that amendment that would be endorsed by the Court more than a half-century later in *Brown v. Board of Education.*

Justice John Marshall Harlan helped pave the way for Brown v. Board of Education *when he dissented from the majority opinion in* Plessy v. Ferguson.

The white race deems itself to be the dominant race in this country. And so it is, in prestige, in achievements, in education, in wealth and in power. . . . But in view of the Constitution, in the eye of the law, there is in this country no superior, dominant, ruling class of citizens. There is no caste here. Our Constitution is color-blind, and neither knows nor tolerates classes among citizens. In respect of civil rights, all citizens are equal before the law. The humblest is the peer of the most powerful. The law regards man as man, and takes no account of his surroundings or of his color when his civil rights as guaranteed by the supreme law of the land are involved. It is, therefore, to be regretted that this high tribunal, the final expositor of the fundamental law of the land, has reached the conclusion that it is competent for a state to regulate the enjoyment by citizens of their civil rights solely upon the basis of race.

concluded his opinion by stating, "If one race be inferior to the other socially, the Constitution of the United States cannot put them upon the same plane."

The Court's opinion in *Plessy v. Ferguson* began a national policy known as "separate but equal": The law could mandate

Public facilities were rigidly segregated during the Jim Crow era. Reminders of racism marked public buildings everywhere.

separate public facilities for white and black citizens, but the facilities must be of equal quality. Jim Crow laws remained firmly in place; indeed, during the years following the *Plessy* decision, more Jim Crow legislation was put on the books. Georgia passed a separate-park law. Lawmakers in Baltimore and other Southern cities passed laws prohibiting blacks from living in certain neighborhoods. Golf courses, barbershops and beauty parlors, sports arenas, and other businesses and facilities serving the public became rigidly segregated. And communities in the South continued to operate Jim Crow schools.

Chapter 2

School Segregation

At the start of the twentieth century, nowhere was segregation in American society more obvious—and arguably more damaging—than in the public schools. Particularly in the South, school systems were rigidly divided—one school for white children and one for black. Although the *Plessy v. Ferguson* decision of 1896 suggested that racially segregated public facilities must be of equal quality, schools for black students were rarely on par with schools for whites. Supreme Court rulings on segregated schools during the first quarter of the twentieth century did little to improve these educational inequities. Not until the late 1930s did the Supreme Court begin to address the problem of separate and unequal American schools.

The Development of Public Schools

Free public education, financed by tax dollars, did not become widely available throughout the United States until after the Civil War. After the war, as the nation moved from a farming-based economy to a manufacturing economy, the country's political, business, and educational leaders saw the need for all children to attend school for several years to learn reading, writing, mathematics, and other basic skills necessary to cope with a modern economy. In the North, public education was substantially further advanced than in the South, where only the children of the wealthy were able to attend school. During the 1870s, education in the South expanded rapidly, but Southern schools, as well as some in the North, did not enroll black children.

The task of educating the South's former slaves and their children after the Civil War fell to the Freedman's Bureau, an entity created by an act of Congress in 1865 to provide food, shelter, medical care, and education to the freed slaves. The task of educating the former slaves was a formidable one. Only a very small percentage of slaves were taught to read and write. In some Southern states, teaching slaves to read or write had been against the law, because many slave owners realized that literate slaves were more likely than their illiterate counterparts to oppose their predicament and demand their civil rights. The Freedman's Bureau set up more than four thousand rudimentary schools throughout the South, and by 1870 about 25 percent of school-age ex-slaves were attending schools.

The Freedman's Bureau went out of existence in 1872, but many of the schools for black children that it established remained in existence, eventually financed by state and local tax dollars. Rather than allowing black children to enroll in the new public schools that were appearing throughout the South, the

The inequities of racism were most apparent in the segregated public schools. The schools for black students were usually grossly inferior to those for white students.

states of the old Confederacy preferred to finance separate schools for black children. Some Southern states passed laws segregating the schools. In the North and West, integrated schools were more common, though some school districts remained stubbornly segregated. At one time or another, twenty-five states had school segregation laws on the books. And as late as 1945, seventeen states still operated segregated school systems.

American public education continued to develop during the twentieth century. In 1890 only 4 percent of high school–age youngsters in the United States attended school. By 1930 that number had risen to almost 50 percent. By 1918 every state had passed a mandatory school attendance law. During this time period, schools became increasingly more sophisticated, as state and local boards of education regularized curriculum and monitored facilities and instructors; by 1920 the one-room schoolhouse was, for the most part, an artifact of the past. Nonetheless, for blacks, especially those who lived in the South, education remained rudimentary and grossly inferior. In *The Souls of Black Folk,* his 1903 study of African American life at the turn of the century, W. E. B. Du Bois, the noted author and civil rights leader, summed up the conditions of America's Jim Crow schools:

> The Negro colleges, hurriedly founded, were inadequately equipped, illogically distributed, and of varying efficiency and grade; the normal and high schools were doing little more than common-school work, and the common schools were training but a third of the children who ought to be in them, and training these too often poorly.

Segregated schools were always separate but never equal. During the first three decades of the twentieth century, state and local governments poured more and more money into developing their school systems, but schools established for black students received only a pittance of these expenditures. In 1910, for example, in eleven Southern states with segregated schools, $9.45 was spent per year to educate each white child, while only $2.90 was spent on each black child. By 1916 the expenditure for

An 1890 photo shows a grammar school for white male students. In general, white students benefited from better facilities, educational materials, and teachers.

white students in these states had increased to $10.32, while the money spent on black students had actually decreased to $2.89.

The black schools were inferior in almost every way. The buildings were dilapidated. Many lacked adequate heating systems; and even by the 1930s, when indoor plumbing and electricity were commonplace, schools for black children lacked these basic necessities. The classrooms in black schools were frequently overcrowded, and the teachers were paid considerably less than their colleagues teaching in white schools. Students attending white schools were offered more subjects and extracurricular activities than their counterparts attending black schools. Schools for blacks, particularly in the rural South, were often located in hard-to-reach areas, and students were rarely provided with transportation to and from school each day. As might be expected, the dropout rate in black schools was high, and the literacy rate among African Americans remained disturbingly low, even fifty years after slavery had become extinct.

Over time the Jim Crow schools did improve, mainly because of the dedication of the African American teachers who struggled to make the best of difficult circumstances and the efforts of inspired black students who saw that education was the gateway to a better life. Nonetheless, even as late as 1945, the situation for black students attending segregated schools in the South was appalling. The South spent half as much on its black students as it spent on whites. Teachers at black schools received salaries that were 30 percent less than those of their white counterparts. States with segregated schools spent $42 million each year to bus white children to schools, while these same states spent only $1 million transporting black children to their schools.

Inferior schools were the passageway to an inferior life. Poorly educated, blacks could not have access to the jobs that lifted them out of poverty. They could not secure decent housing. They could not obtain needed medical care when illness struck. They lived in a separate and unequal world from white Americans.

Challenging Jim Crow Education

Did not separate and unequal public schooling violate the precedent set in the *Plessy v. Ferguson* case, which stressed that segregated public facilities must be of equal quality? It would seem so, but legal challenges to Jim Crow education received no sympathy from the Supreme Court until the late 1930s. Three school segregation cases that reached the Supreme Court between 1899 and 1927 did nothing to dismantle the educational color barrier that separated white and black students.

In 1899 a school segregation case titled *Cumming v. Richmond County Board of Education* came before the Supreme Court for a ruling. The case concerned the board of education in Richmond County, Georgia, which had provided separate grammar schools for white and black students as well as separate high schools for white male students, white female students, and black students. By the late 1890s, the grammar school for black children had become overcrowded, and the Richmond County school board solved the problem by closing the black high school and using it for black grammar school students. The parents of black high school students were told to urge their churches to establish schools for black high schoolers. A group of parents filed a lawsuit against the school board, maintaining that, in light of the recent *Plessy v. Ferguson* ruling, the school board should be required to close the high school for whites as well so that all children, white and black, would have equal educational opportunities.

Justice John Marshall Harlan, who had dissented so vigorously in the *Plessy v. Ferguson* case, delivered the Court's unanimous decision in *Cumming v. Richmond County Board of Education.* Although Harlan granted that "the benefits and burdens of public taxation must be shared by citizens with-

In Cumming v. Richmond County Board of Education, *Justice John Marshall Harlan supported the view that public education was a matter belonging to the states, not the federal government.*

out discrimination against any class on account of their race," he asserted that "the education of people in schools maintained by state taxation is a matter belonging to the respective states, and any interference on the part of Federal authority with the management of such schools cannot be justified." Hence, the high school for white students could remain open, and black students would be made to forgo the benefits of a high school education.

For the opponents of segregated schools, the Court's decision in the 1908 case of *Berea College v. Kentucky* was perhaps even more troubling than its ruling in *Cumming v. Richmond County.* Berea College of Kentucky, established in 1859, was one of the few unsegregated Southern colleges. In the wake of the *Plessy v. Ferguson* ruling, Kentucky passed a law mandating that an educational institution could enroll students of both races only if the classes for whites were held separately from those for black students. In addition, the classes for whites and blacks had to be conducted at least twenty-five miles apart. Berea College, a private institution not supported by Kentucky's tax dollars, sued the state. The college's administration argued that the school had been founded "to promote the cause of Christ"; hence, Kentucky's law denied the free practice of religion, a right guaranteed by the First Amendment to the Constitution.

Kentucky's Supreme Court ruled against Berea College, though it judged that the twenty-five-mile requirement of Kentucky's law was somewhat excessive. Berea College was ordered to segregate its classes. Not satisfied, the school appealed its case to the Supreme Court. The High Court, however, supported the ruling of the lower court. Since Berea College had received a corporate charter from the state of Kentucky, the Court reasoned, it was obligated to obey the laws of Kentucky. Moreover, the Court felt that the law's mandate that classes be racially segregated did not substantially affect Berea College's mission. Thus, school segregation could be forced upon an institution even if that institution preferred to be integrated.

A third Supreme Court ruling in 1927 further solidified the notion that segregated schools were constitutionally on firm footing. The case involved Martha Lum, a nine-year-old Chinese American girl living in Bolivar County, Mississippi. Aware of the deplorable conditions of the local school for black children, Martha's father, Gong Lum, attempted to enroll her in the white school in his neighborhood. The local school board denied her request to register, and Mr. Lum took his case to court. On appeal, the Supreme Court heard his case. The Lums were not directly questioning the constitutionality of segregated schools; they were merely trying to get Martha classified as white so that she could attend a superior school. The Court, using the *Cumming v. Richmond County* case as a precedent, ruled that the federal government had no business trying to regulate Mississippi's school system. "The right and power of the state to regulate the method of providing for the education of its youth at public expense is clear," wrote Chief Justice William Howard Taft.

These three Supreme Court rulings suggested that segregated schooling would remain a part of American life for many years to come. Bowing to the precedent established by *Plessy v.*

Although a strong opponent of segregation, W. E. B. Du Bois advocated improving black schools rather than fighting for integration.

Ferguson in 1896, the Court had acknowledged the legality of segregated public facilities. The Court had also firmly established the notion that the federal government must not interfere with the way an individual state or local school board maintained its schools. Examining the situation in an essay in 1935, W. E. B. Du Bois, a strong opponent of segregation of any kind, acknowledged that those who fought for integrated schools were engaged in a losing battle. Instead, reasoned Du Bois, African American leaders should focus on vastly improving the black schools so that no African American child would receive an inferior education.

The First Victories

While Du Bois was quite reasonably suggesting that any effort to integrate schools was hopeless, two brilliant African American lawyers, Charles Houston and Thurgood Marshall, were working on a case that would prove the great civil rights leader wrong. Houston was the dean of the law school at Howard University, a college in Washington, D.C., founded specifically for African American students just after the Civil War. Besides performing his significant duties at Howard University, Houston, a graduate of Harvard University School of Law, also occasionally handled a courtroom case. His specialty was civil rights law.

Thurgood Marshall, a product of Baltimore's segregated public schools, was one of Howard University School of Law's top graduates. After graduating from Howard in 1933, Marshall

MR. CIVIL RIGHTS

Thurgood Marshall had working-class roots. His father, William, worked as a dining-car waiter for the Baltimore & Ohio Railroad, and his mother, Norma, was a homemaker and later a teacher. The family lived in a section of Baltimore dominated by neatly maintained brick rowhouses, and the Marshall boys attended segregated schools. But Mr. and Mrs. Marshall believed that their two sons, Aubery and Thoroughgood (later shortened to Thurgood), could aspire to higher goals, even at a time when opportunities for the brightest black children were limited. Aubery attended Lincoln University, a traditionally black college in Pennsylvania, went on to medical school, and became a physician specializing in the treatment of tuberculosis, a lung disease that claimed many lives during the first half of the twentieth century.

Thurgood also attended Lincoln University, and upon graduation he decided to study law. His application to the law school at the University of Maryland was rejected because the institution did not enroll black students, regardless of their talents and intelligence. So Thurgood earned his law degree at Howard University in Washington, D.C., graduating first in his class in 1933.

After passing the bar exam, Marshall set up practice in Baltimore. He was recruited by the local chapter of the NAACP to work on some civil rights cases, and soon he was working with his old Howard University mentor, Charles Houston, on important civil rights cases. In 1934 Marshall assisted Houston in preparing a lawsuit on behalf of nine African American students who had been turned down by the University of Maryland School of Law. In 1936 an appeals court ordered the university to admit the nine students, the first of a long series of school-desegregation victories in which Marshall participated. In 1939 Marshall quit his private practice to work full-time for the NAACP's Legal Defense Fund. There Marshall hired a talented team of attorneys who would spearhead the lawsuit known as *Brown v. Board of Education of Topeka, Kansas*. In 1954 the Supreme Court's decision in *Brown v. Board of Education* outlawed racial segregation in America's public schools. Marshall argued thirty-two cases before the High Court and emerged victorious twenty-nine times.

In 1961 President John Kennedy named Marshall to the U.S. Court of Appeals. Six years later, President Lyndon Johnson named Marshall as the first African American justice to serve on the Supreme Court. Marshall served on the High Court until 1991.

During his lifetime, Marshall, one of the giants of twentieth-century American history, received many awards. Perhaps none was more appreciated than the tribute that came from the University of Maryland School of Law. Many years after the school rejected Marshall's application, it bestowed his name upon its law library.

Marshall died in 1993, at the age of eighty-four.

THE NATIONAL ASSOCIATION FOR THE ADVANCEMENT OF COLORED PEOPLE

In 1905, W. E. B. Du Bois gathered a group of civil rights leaders for a conference in New York City. Du Bois and his followers formed the Niagara Movement, an organization dedicated to extending the civil rights of black Americans. The Niagara Movement was essentially a failure, but in 1909 Du Bois, undaunted, formed a new civil rights organization named the National Association for the Advancement of Colored People, whose goal was "to achieve, through peaceful and lawful means, equal citizenship rights for all American citizens by eliminating segregation and discrimination in housing, employment, voting, schools, the courts, transportation, recreation." Moorfield Storey, a white Boston lawyer, became the NAACP's first president, and Du Bois took the post of director of publicity and research. The new organization was an immediate success. Within five years, fifty NAACP chapters had formed across the United States.

One of Du Bois's major accomplishments was establishing the NAACP's scholarly journal, the *Crisis*. Scholars from around the country contributed articles to the *Crisis*, which became the foremost civil rights publication in the United States. The NAACP also published a series of books and pamphlets on various civil rights issues, such as *Thirty Years of Lynching in the United States, 1889–1918*.

In 1939 the NAACP formed its Legal Defense Fund, an entity established to fight racial discrimination through the courts. During the 1940s "Inc. Fund," as it was commonly called, recruited some of the best attorneys in the country to wage the legal battle against school segregation that culminated in victory in the lawsuit titled *Brown v. Board of Education of Topeka, Kansas*.

Today, the NAACP has five hundred thousand members and eighteen hundred chapters across the United States.

---

treatment under the law. Marshall presented, as precedent, a California court's ruling in the case of an Indian child who had been denied admission to a public school even though there was no public school available for Indian children. The court ordered the local school board to open a school for Native American children or admit the child to its all-white school.

On June 25, 1935, Judge Eugene O'Dunne of the Baltimore City Court handed down his decision: The University of Maryland law school must admit Donald Murray. O'Dunne's ruling was upheld by the Maryland Court of Appeals in January 1936.

The University of Maryland chose not to appeal the decision to the Supreme Court, and Murray enrolled in the institution as ordered by the court.

That same summer Lloyd Lionel Gaines, a black student from Missouri, had applied to his state's segregated law school and had been turned down solely because of his race. Again Charles Houston took up his cause, but this time the Missouri court that heard the case ruled against the plaintiff. Houston appealed to the U.S. Supreme Court. The Court heard the case, which became known as *Gaines v. Canada*, on November 9, 1938. A month later the Court handed down a ruling that became another important victory for Charles Houston and other opponents of segregated schools.

The University of Missouri School of Law was forced to open its doors to Lloyd Gaines. The Court ruled that Missouri "excludes negroes from the advantages of the law school it has established at the University of Missouri." The law separating the races in schools "rests wholly upon the equality of the privileges

Donald Murray (center) enrolled in the University of Maryland law school in 1936, after Marshall (left) and Houston (right) successfully argued his case.

which the laws give to the separated groups within the State." Since Missouri did not have a law school for black students, it must admit blacks to its law school.

The victories in the *Murray* and *Gaines* cases prompted the NAACP to take more assertive action. In 1939 the organization established the NAACP Legal Defense Fund, with Thurgood Marshall as chief counsel. The fund's main purpose was simple: to fight civil rights battles in the nation's courtrooms and thereby improve the plight of all aspects of African American life—education, housing, politics, employment, transportation, entertainment.

Marshall went right to work. In 1939 he took a Maryland county school board to court for paying its black teachers one-third less than their white colleagues. Marshall won, and black teachers across the entire state of Maryland celebrated a healthy raise. Victorious in Maryland, Marshall, the following year, filed substantially the same lawsuit across the border in Virginia, where he lost in a local court but won a reversal in a court of appeals.

By this time Marshall was gaining a national reputation. He became known as "Mr. Civil Rights," a brilliant and tireless lawyer who roamed the nation fighting key civil rights battles in court. He defended blacks accused of crimes. He argued highly technical cases involving subtle aspects of constitutional law. Often he conducted his business in the courtrooms of small Southern towns where the local citizens did not take a liking to brilliant black men who fought for the legal and civil rights of beaten-down black citizens. But Marshall was fearless, shaking off threats on his life with a joke or an amusing anecdote.

Perhaps because of the efforts of Marshall and Houston, the entire legal climate in the United States began to change in issues involving race. In 1939 James Nabrit, a professor at Howard University School of Law, argued an Oklahoma law preventing blacks from voting before the Supreme Court in a case titled *Lane v. Wilson*. By a 6-2 majority, the Court ruled that the Oklahoma law violated the Fifteenth Amendment to the Constitution, which guaranteed citizens their right to vote. In 1941, in *Mitchell v. United States*, the Court struck down an Arkansas transportation law that forced blacks to travel in train cars without toilets and running water. In 1944, in a case titled *Smith v. Allwright*, argued by Thurgood Marshall, the Court struck down a Texas law that had prohibited black citizens from voting in primary elections. In 1946 Marshall again appeared before the Supreme Court, arguing on behalf of a black Virginia woman named Irene Morgan who had refused to sit in the back of a bus bound for Baltimore and was arrested and fined ten dollars. The Court ruled, in *Morgan v. Virginia*, that state transportation laws could not be applied in interstate travel.

Sweatt and McLaurin

Before the end of the 1940s, Marshall took up the cases of two other students seeking graduate-level education in states with segregated universities. Herman Marion Sweatt, a Texas mailman, had applied to the law school at the University of Texas and been turned down, solely because he was black. Sweatt sued the university, and a county court ordered the state of Texas either to admit Sweatt to its law school or open a separate law school of equal quality for black students. The state chose to open a new law school for blacks. The Prairie View Law School opened with a few rented rooms in Houston, a faculty consisting of two professors, and no law library. The county court found that arrangement acceptable, but Sweatt pressed his case further. Marshall took his case to an appeals court, promising "a real showdown fight against Jim Crow education." Their opponent was Theophilus Shickel Painter, president of the University of Texas, and their courtroom battle became known as *Sweatt v. Painter*.

Marshall had the fight of his life. Before the appeals court heard the case, Painter had announced the creation of a brand-new law school for black students, one substantially bigger and better equipped and staffed than the makeshift Prairie View school. The university's sharp and polished lawyers argued that the case was merely being fought for the benefit of the NAACP, not because the plaintiff really desired a legal education. Marshall called as an expert witness Professor Robert Redfield, chairman of the anthropology department at the prestigious University of Chicago, who testified that black students, contrary to widespread opinion, had the same intellectual potential as white students and would attain the same academic achievements if they had equal educational opportunities.

Marshall lost the case. The appeals court ruled that the state of Texas was complying with the law by offering Sweatt admission to its new law school for black students. Sweatt went back to delivering mail, and Marshall took his case to the Supreme Court, which would take three years to hear Sweatt's case.

While *Sweatt v. Painter* was awaiting its day in the Supreme Court, Marshall accepted the case of George W. McLaurin, a sixty-eight-year-old teacher who applied to the University of Oklahoma's doctoral program in education. McLaurin was rejected because he was black. McLaurin and Marshall filed a lawsuit in U.S. district court, which ordered the university to admit the plaintiff. Oklahoma complied but made McLaurin pay for his courtroom victory. In class, he was forced to sit in a separate row of seats marked "Reserved for Colored." He was restricted to a single table in the library and was made to eat his

Although George W. McLaurin's courtroom victory allowed him to participate in the University of Oklahoma's doctoral program, he was forced to sit apart from his white fellow students.

lunch at a separate cafeteria table. When Marshall made these conditions known to the district court that had ordered the university to admit McLaurin, he obtained no relief. Marshall appealed to the Supreme Court, which heard the appeals by McLaurin and Sweatt on the same day in April 1950.

A Double Victory

On June 5, 1950, the Supreme Court gave Thurgood Marshall and the opponents of segregated schooling a double victory. In the *Sweatt v. Painter* case, the Court ruled that the new law school for Texas's black students did not provide a "legal education equivalent to that offered by the state to students of other races." Chief Justice Fred M. Vinson, writing for a unanimous Court, asserted in his written opinion that the new law school lacked the important but hard-to-measure qualities of great law schools: "Such qualities, to name but a few, include reputation of the faculty, experience of the administration, position and influence of the alumni, standing in the community, traditions and prestige." The Court ordered Sweatt admitted to the University of Texas School of Law. The victory was, thus far, Marshall's greatest. In the cases of *Murray v. Maryland* and *Gaines v. Canada*, Marshall had won admission to all-white law schools in states where no law school had existed for black students. In *Sweatt v. Painter*, he convinced the Supreme Court to order the admission of a student to an all-white law school even though a law school did exist for black students.

In *McLaurin v. Oklahoma State Regents for Higher Education*, the Court ruled that the restrictions placed upon the plaintiff by the university "impair and inhibit his ability to study, to engage in discussion and exchange views with other students, and in general, to learn his profession." Chief Justice Vinson also asserted that if McLaurin could not receive an equal education at the University of Oklahoma because of the restrictions placed upon him, those students whom he would later teach "will necessarily suffer to the extent that his training is unequal to that of his classmates." McLaurin was allowed to matriculate at the University of Oklahoma under the same conditions as his fellow students who happened to be white.

The written opinions of Chief Justice Fred M. Vinson were instrumental in ending segregated schooling.

Thus, at the midpoint of the twentieth century, the opponents of segregated education were making some progress. They had, at least, convinced the Supreme Court to allow black students to enroll in white-only universities in states that did not provide equal facilities for black students. On several occasions, the Court had asserted that if the educational facilities were separate, then they must be of equal quality. After 1950 Thurgood Marshall would take his fight to end segregated schooling in a bold new direction. He would try to prove that no segregated school, regardless of its facilities, curriculum, and staffing, could provide its students with a quality education.

Chapter 3

Four Lawsuits

WORLD WAR II BROUGHT the promise of positive change for America's black citizens. The United States had helped defeat a European leader, Adolf Hitler, who had persecuted citizens because of their ethnic backgrounds. During the 1930s and 1940s, Hitler had imprisoned and executed six million European Jews and six million Slavs and other people whom he considered ethnically inferior to his so-called German master race. After the war many Americans, who found Hitler's racial policies repugnant, would turn a critical eye on their own society, which still discriminated against American citizens who were not white. Moreover, thousands of African American soldiers had distinguished themselves in battle during the war; those who had put their lives on the line and returned home safely surely deserved to enjoy all the benefits of American citizenship without restriction.

Indeed, soon after the war ended in 1945, some of the discriminatory barriers that separated the races in America began to come down. In August 1945, a few weeks after the war ended, the Brooklyn Dodgers signed a fleet-footed infielder and army veteran named Jackie Robinson to their minor league team in Montreal. Two seasons later, when he made his Brooklyn debut, Robinson became the first black player in the twentieth century to play major league baseball. Robinson excelled on the field with his spirited play, and soon other major league teams began signing talented African American players. Major league baseball, which had been for whites only since the time of *Plessy v. Ferguson*, rapidly integrated.

Jackie Robinson stunned the world when he became the first black to play on a major league baseball team.

A year after Robinson broke baseball's color barrier, President Harry Truman issued an executive order integrating the U.S. armed services. Prior to that point, the American armed forces had operated separate regiments for white and black soldiers, sailors, and airmen.

Encouraged by these events, and by the school segregation cases won by Thurgood Marshall and Charles Houston during the 1930s and 1940s, the NAACP embarked in a bold new direction in its effort to desegregate America's public schools. The NAACP had won lawsuits in the *Murray v. Maryland, Gaines v. Canada,* and *Sweatt v. Painter* cases because it had proved that states had not provided educational facilities for black citizens or had provided facilities that were unquestionably inferior in quality. Now, in late 1950, the NAACP attempted a new strategy. It would begin to challenge the "separate" part of the "separate but equal" doctrine established by *Plessy v. Ferguson* in 1896.

The NAACP would begin to argue that segregating black children in separate schools, regardless of the quality of those schools, led to an inferior education; hence, forcing black children to attend a segregated school violated their right to equal protection of the law guaranteed by the Fourteenth Amendment to the Constitution.

In the early 1950s, the NAACP spearheaded four lawsuits involving segregated schools—in Clarendon County, South Carolina; Prince Edward County, Virginia; Claymont and Hockessin, Delaware; and Topeka, Kansas. These lawsuits became the basis for the landmark 1954 Supreme Court case of *Brown v. Board of Education of Topeka, Kansas.*

Briggs v. Elliott

The *Briggs v. Elliott* case began in 1947 as an argument over a school bus. The school board in Clarendon County, South Carolina, provided thirty-four buses to transport white students to their schools; no bus was available for black students. Not surprisingly, many black students became truants and dropouts; and as a direct result, about one-third of the county's black citizens were illiterate. Joseph Albert DeLaine, a Clarendon County minister and principal of a school for black students, asked the county school board chairman, R. W. Elliott, to purchase buses for black children. When the school board denied the request, DeLaine and others filed a lawsuit.

On June 8, 1948, the lawsuit was thrown out of court on a technicality: Levi Pearson, the plaintiff identified in the lawsuit, lived on the property line between two school districts and was judged to have no legal standing to file the suit. Pearson, a farmer, immediately had his credit cut off by the local white-owned supply store. When he tried to sell his crops and timber, he could find no buyers. DeLaine fared worse. He and his wife were fired from their jobs. Their house was set on fire, and the fire department watched it burn to the ground. His church was also burned. DeLaine was eventually chased from the county when he was saddled with a trumped-up charge of assault with a deadly weapon.

Thurgood Marshall had become aware of this appalling situation. In March 1949 he met with a group of Clarendon County's black citizens and convinced them to file a lawsuit based on the grossly unequal educational facilities provided for Clarendon County's black students. The school board spent $179 each year to educate each white child and only $43 on each black child. The white schools had one teacher per twenty-eight students; the black schools averaged one teacher per forty-seven students. The black schools lacked indoor plumbing; the students relieved themselves in outhouses and drank water from metal buckets. Black students were assessed fees for textbooks and heating coal, while the white students attended school for free. It took Marshall until November to convince twenty black citizens of Clarendon County to sign a petition to file a lawsuit against school board chairman R. W. Elliott. The first name on the petition was Harry Briggs, a gas station attendant, a navy veteran, and a father of five school-age children. The case became known as *Briggs v. Elliott.*

Briggs v. Elliott began in U.S. district court in Charleston, South Carolina, on May 28, 1951. That morning several hundred black citizens arrived at the majestic Victorian-style courtroom to hear the great Thurgood Marshall argue his case before a panel of three federal judges.

The school board's lawyer, Robert Figg, surprised Marshall. Figg admitted that the educational facilities for Clarendon County's black students were surely inferior. He informed the court that the governor was presently proposing sweeping legislation and significant expenditures that would remedy the situation. But Marshall wanted nothing of appeasement. He did not want his clients' children to wait another few years for the state of South Carolina to provide relief. He called nationally known educators as expert witnesses to testify to the deplorable conditions of Clarendon County's black schools—conditions that needed to be remedied immediately, not two or three years down the road. Furthermore, Marshall was taking the case one step further: He would try to prove that segregated schools of any kind, regardless of quality, provided black children with an inferior education.

To this end, Marshall's assistant, Robert Carter, another brilliant Howard University law school alumnus, called Kenneth Clark to the witness stand. Clark, a nationally known educational psychologist, testified to the damaging effects of segregation on schoolchildren: "I have reached the conclusion from the examination of my own results and from an examination of the literature in the entire field that discrimination, prejudice and segregation have definitely detrimental effects on the personality development of the Negro child." He added that the black Clarendon County schoolchildren whom he examined exhibited "basic feelings of inferiority, conflict, confusion in his self-image, resentment, hostility towards whites," and other personality

KENNETH CLARK'S DOLL TESTS

Psychologist Kenneth Clark had an unusual way of conducting research. To determine the effects of segregation on black children, Clark used dolls. He would show a child a black doll and a white doll and ask the child which doll he or she liked best, which doll was nicer, which doll was more fun to play with. Clark, who held a Ph.D. from Columbia University and began his research in the late 1930s, was very disturbed with the results. More often than not, black children identified the white doll as being nicer and more fun to play with. Clark concluded, therefore, that black children, even youngsters three or four years old, had already developed a negative self-image. He reasoned that their disliking of the black dolls indicated their dissatisfaction with their own racial background, a dissatisfaction resulting from living in a segregated society that judged black people as inferiors.

To prepare for his crucial testimony in the *Briggs v. Elliott* case, Clark had examined sixteen black children from Clarendon County. Of the sixteen, eleven judged the black doll as the bad doll. Ten children referred to the white doll as the nicer doll. From this evidence, as well as research conducted during his two-decade professional career, Clark concluded that "these children, in Clarendon County, like other human beings who are subjected to an obviously inferior status in which they live, have been definitely harmed in the development of their personalities; that the signs of instability in their personalities are clear, and I think that every psychologist would accept and interpret these signs as such."

In 1953, Clark summarized his findings in the book *Desegregation: An Appraisal of the Evidence.*

problems. Several more expert witnesses corroborated Clark's testimony. Figg called only a few witnesses, who testified that mixing white and black children in the same schools would cause social unrest and other problems.

Testimony continued for a day and a half. Throughout the proceedings, the courtroom was packed with black spectators, mostly country folks who had never seen a courtroom in their lives but who now sensed the importance of the issue being discussed. They had also come to see Thurgood Marshall and his talented associates in action—articulate black lawyers addressing white judges and lawyers in a Southern courtroom.

After the witnesses had been examined and cross-examined, Marshall made his summary remarks to the court. "The Negro child is made to go to an inferior school; he is branded in his own mind as inferior," asserted Marshall. "This sets up a roadblock in his mind which prevents his ever feeling he is equal. You can teach such a child the Constitution, anthropology, and citizenship, but he knows it isn't true." Marshall accused the Clarendon County school board of doing something unlawful by segregat-

After conducting much research, psychologist Kenneth Clark concluded that segregation was detrimental to black children. His findings were cited in Briggs v. Elliott.

AN AMERICAN DILEMMA

One of the twentieth century's most influential books on African Americans was written by a Swede. In 1944, after several years of research, Gunnar Myrdal, a social economist, published a detailed study of African American life titled *An American Dilemma*. Myrdal and his assistants on the project had gathered data for their study by traveling around the entire United States, attending conferences, church services, and political rallies; discussing his subject with politicians, businessmen, and educators; and interviewing hundreds of ordinary working folks.

An American Dilemma presents a devastating attack on a nation supposedly committed to democracy and justice. The book's scope is wide and its indictments sweeping. Economically, most black Americans, in both the North and

Gunnar Myrdal, author of An American Dilemma.

South, lived in or near poverty; and since their schools were generally inadequate, they had little hope of rising even to the middle class. Politically, too many blacks were voiceless, lacking access to the ballot box in the South and lacking the education to use it wisely in the North. Medically, the African American's predicament was appalling; their average lifespan was well below that of white Americans, and the infant and child mortality rates for black Americans were astronomically high. Socially, the American Negro lived as an outsider, unable to enjoy, because of segregation or economic circumstance, the enrichment afforded by the arts, travel, and the world of entertainment.

Although Myrdal did not testify in the school desegregation cases, his book provided the opponents of segregated schools with substantial evidence to defend their cause. More importantly, his book was read by the Supreme Court justices who would eventually decide on the legality of Jim Crow schooling.

ing its schools, and he concluded by suggesting the obvious remedy: "There is no relief for the Negro children of Clarendon County except to be permitted to attend existing and superior white schools."

Although defeated in Briggs v. Elliott, *Thurgood Marshall remained firm in his resolve to fight the barriers separating blacks and whites.*

Marshall lost his case. Three weeks later, the court ruled that since segregated schools have existed for more than seventy-five years, "it is a late day to say that such segregation is violative of fundamental constitutional rights." But the court did order the county to equalize the two school systems as soon as practical. And one of the three judges dissented. In his dissenting opinion, Judge J. Waites Waring called segregated schooling "an evil that must be eradicated," and said that "the place to stop it is in the first grade and not in graduate colleges."

Marshall was beaten but not defeated. He would appeal the decision to the Supreme Court.

Brown v. Board of Education of Topeka, Kansas

A few days after the *Briggs v. Elliott* decision had been rendered, a federal district court in Topeka, Kansas, began hearing another school segregation case. This one included a man named Oliver Brown and his seven-year-old daughter, Linda. Each school day Linda had to cross a set of railroad tracks and board a bus to take her to the "colored" school on the other side of Topeka, even though a school for white children was located only a few blocks from her home. Brown joined a group of Topeka's African American citizens who had been trying for three years to convince the board of education to improve the schools designated for black students. Exasperated after several unsuccessful attempts, the group finally filed a lawsuit with Oliver Brown's name atop the list of plaintiffs.

Thurgood Marshall was still busy with the Clarendon County case, so he sent two of his capable assistants, Robert Carter and Jack Greenberg, to handle the case, which began in a half-filled Topeka courtroom on June 25, 1951. Carter and Greenberg summoned to the witness stand a handful of the plaintiffs—children included—who testified on the difficulties they encountered each day traveling to the "colored" schools. Linda Brown's commute to school, for example, began at 7:40 A.M., but she did not arrive at school until nine o'clock.

Then Jack Greenberg called to the witness stand Hugh Speer, chairman of the department of education at the University of Kansas. Speer corroborated the point made by Kenneth Clark in the *Briggs v. Elliott* trial:

> If the colored children are denied the experience of associating with white children, who represent 90 percent of our national society in which these colored children must live, then the colored child's curriculum is being greatly curtailed. The Topeka curriculum or any school curriculum cannot be equal under segregation.

Several other witnesses concurred. But the most telling point was made by Louisa Holt, an assistant professor in the psychology department at Kansas University. Holt agreed that segregated schooling impairs a black child's education, but she added a crucial point about segregated schools not made by other witnesses:

> The fact that it is enforced, that it is legal, I think, has more importance than the mere fact of segregation by itself does because this gives legal and official sanction

to a policy which is inevitably interpreted both by white people and by Negroes as denoting the inferiority of the Negro group.

The NAACP lost this case too. The court found that Topeka's segregated schools were, for the most part, of comparable quality; hence, the constitutional rights of black students were not being violated. Nonetheless, the court's opinion acknowledged a point that would be useful when the case was appealed to the Supreme Court:

> Segregation of white and colored children in public schools has a detrimental effect upon the colored children. The impact is greater when it has the sanction of the law; for the policy of separating the races is usually interpreted as denoting the inferiority of the Negro group.

The Delaware Cases

In the spring of 1951, two lawsuits were filed in the U.S. district court in Wilmington, Delaware, against the members of the state's board of education. One suit was brought forth by Ethel Belton and other black citizens of Claymont, who charged the state with providing an inferior education for their children. A similar suit was filed by Sara Bulah and other black citizens of nearby Hockessin. The two cases were titled *Belton v. Gebhart* and *Bulah v. Gebhart*—Francis Gebhart was a member of the board of education—and had their day in court on October 22, 1951.

Jack Greenberg and Louis Redding, of the NAACP's Wilmington chapter, handled the case. They called witnesses to testify on the deplorable conditions of the schools for black students. One school for black children had no gymnasium, no nurse's office, and no water fountains. A single toilet accommodated the entire school—students and teachers alike. As in the previous segregation cases, an expert witness testified to the damage that segregated schooling inflicted upon black children. Frederic Wertham, a nationally known psychologist and author, testified that even if the black schools hired brilliant teachers like the great physicist Albert Einstein, those schools still would provide an inferior education: "It is the fact of segregation in general and the problems that come out of it that to my mind is anti-educational." According to Wertham, segregation caused in a young child "an unsolvable emotional conflict" that damages the child's ability to learn and become a productive adult.

Though the NAACP's tactics in the Delaware cases were similar to those used in South Carolina and Kansas, the results were different. The NAACP won the Delaware lawsuit. In early April 1952 Judge Collins Seitz delivered an opinion that sharply criticized the state of Delaware for the way it was treating black students. He agreed with Frederic Wertham's assessment of the damage that segregated schools caused black children. Seitz asserted that "the 'separate but equal' doctrine in education should be rejected," though he granted that its rejection must come from the Supreme Court. Seitz concluded his opinion with an order that Thurgood Marshall called "the first real victory in our campaign to destroy segregation of American pupils in elementary and high schools." Rather than order the school board to improve Delaware's black schools, Seitz ordered that the children of the eleven plaintiffs named in the two lawsuits must be immediately admitted to local whites-only schools. The desegregation of Southern elementary and high schools had officially begun.

Davis v. County School Board of Prince Edward County

On May 23, 1951, Spottswood Robinson, a lawyer with the NAACP Legal Defense Fund, filed a lawsuit on behalf of 117 African American students at Robert R. Moton High School in Prince Edward County, Virginia. The suit, the result of a two-week strike by all 450 students, charged the county with providing Moton's pupils with an inferior education. For relief, the plaintiffs asked not for improvements to Moton High or a new high school for black students, but for the immediate desegregation of Prince Edward County's schools. The first name on the list of petitioners was that of Dorothy Davis, a fourteen-year-old freshman, and the case was recorded in district court in Richmond, Virginia, as *Davis v. County School Board of Prince Edward County*.

STRIKE AT MOTON HIGH

The court case titled *Davis v. County School Board of Prince Edward County* was begun by a spirited sixteen-year-old who believed that one committed person can change the world. Barbara Rose Johns, a junior at the all-black Robert R. Moton High School in Prince Edward County, Virginia, was dissatisfied with her education. She had taken field trips to the high school for white students and had marveled at its state-of-the-art facilities—a fine library, well-equipped labs and shops, clean facilities with new equipment, and beautiful landscaping. In the autumn of 1950, she began to share her thoughts with her fellow students, who began to urge their parents to seek relief, through Moton's PTA, from the county school board. After six months the PTA had made no progress, so Barbara began to act. On April 23, 1951, she called an assembly of the entire student body and, at the end of a fiery and eloquent speech, announced a strike. Moton's 450 students would refuse to attend class until their school was improved.

The student leaders asked for a meeting with the chairman of the county school board. He refused to address the group until the students returned to class. But two NAACP lawyers, Oliver Hill and Spottswood Robinson, agreed to meet with the striking students. The two lawyers had decided on a prudent course of action: urge the students to return to class but file a lawsuit. When they met Barbara Rose Johns and her lieutenants, however, the two Howard University law school graduates were much impressed with the students' organization, maturity, and zeal. The strike must continue, the students asserted, but the two lawyers were urged to begin legal proceedings immediately.

Barbara Johns, showing the leadership skills of a woman three times her age, quickly worked to unite skeptical parents and teachers behind the students' cause. Barbara knew that their cause was just, and if parents, students, and faculty worked together, they would surely prevail. The press, fascinated by the brave and eloquent high school girl who battled the influential white men on Prince Edward County's school board, followed the strike and put Barbara's picture on the front page of the newspaper.

The strike lasted two weeks. The students agreed to return to school after the NAACP obtained 117 signatures on a petition to desegregate Prince Edward County's white schools. When the strike ended, Barbara's parents, fearing for her safety, sent her to live with relatives in Montgomery, Alabama, to complete her high school education.

The trial commenced on February 25, 1952. The case proceeded in the usual fashion. Spottswood Robinson and Robert Carter brought forth witnesses to testify on the inferiority of Prince Edward County's black schools. Again, a prominent psychologist, M. Brewster Smith, chairman of the psychology department at prestigious Vassar College, testified to the damage caused by legally segregated schools, stating that these schools "make the Negro, on the average, more like the common, prejudiced conception of a Negro, as a stupid, illiterate, apathetic but happy-go-lucky person." Children attending inferior schools, maintained Smith, "are going to grow up with conceptions of themselves as being, in some way, not worthy." Kenneth Clark was also on hand to support Smith's testimony, while the defense's witnesses testified to the great progress that the county was making and would continue to make in Negro education. The defense rested its case with a bold assertion by its lawyer that the entire lawsuit "was fomented by agitation and propaganda by the NAACP." Speaking for the plaintiffs, lawyer

Plaintiffs from Davis v. County School Board of Prince Edward County *stand on the steps of Virginia's capitol.*

Oliver Hill stated that the black students of Moton High "want an opportunity to develop in the business and commerce of this nation," an opportunity not available at Jim Crow schools.

The court sided with the defendants, stating that racial segregation in Virginia was based on "neither prejudice nor caprice" and was merely "a part of the mores of her people." The court's opinion maintained that segregated schools resulted in "no hurt or harm to either race." The students of Moton High were disappointed, but their lawyers promised an appeal to the Supreme Court. In fact, the school year was not quite over when the Supreme Court announced that it would hear appeals in the *Briggs v. Elliott* and *Brown v. Board of Education* cases. Eventually, the Delaware and Prince Edward County cases would be included in the appeal. All four appeals would be heard under the umbrella *Brown v. Board of Education of Topeka, Kansas*. The Court used the Topeka case in the title so that the trial would not appear to concern an issue limited to the South. Indeed, the case would affect the entire country.

Chapter 4

The Supreme Court
Hears the Case

THE CASE TITLED *Brown v. Board of Education of Topeka, Kansas*, was originally scheduled for argument before the U.S. Supreme Court in October 1952. When the Court decided to include the appeals in the Delaware and Prince Edward County cases, the date was pushed back to December. (The Court also agreed to hear, at that time, another school desegregation case titled *Bolling v. Sharpe*, concerning schools in Washington, D.C., but that case would be decided separately, not as part of *Brown v. Board of Education*.) The hearing before the Supreme Court would take three days, and a decision would not be rendered for eighteen months, with a follow-up order of implementation coming a year after that.

Any case that makes its way to the Supreme Court is of great importance. The *Brown v. Board of Education* case would arguably become the most important of the twentieth century.

Preparing the Case

Late in the summer of 1952, the NAACP's sharpest legal minds assembled at the New York City offices of the organization's Legal Defense Fund. There Thurgood Marshall coordinated an intense four-month effort to present the NAACP's argument for school desegregation. Marshall pushed his associates through sixteen-hour days of research as the NAACP's lawyers prepared the legal briefs that would put forth their argument and the courtroom strategy that would attempt to convince the nine justices of the Supreme Court to rule in the NAACP's favor and forever outlaw segregation in public schools.

Marshall and his capable assistants—Robert Carter, Spottswood Robinson, Oliver Hill, Jack Greenberg, and others—scrutinized earlier Supreme Court and lower-court decisions that might serve as legal precedents in the *Brown v. Board of Education* case. They would have to plan a way to refute the Supreme Court's ruling in the *Plessy v. Ferguson* case of 1896. They would have

Thurgood Marshall and his associates spent countless hours researching and preparing the arguments they would present to the Supreme Court in Brown v. Board of Education.

to convince the Court that the rulings on school desegregation handed down during the first part of the twentieth century—*Cumming v. Richmond County Board of Education, Berea College v. Kentucky,* and *Gong Lum v. Rice*—should not govern these recent cases. They would have to present the argument that the most recent school desegregation victories—*Murray v. Maryland, Gaines v. Canada, and Sweatt v. Painter*—suggest that the *Plessy v. Ferguson* decision was losing its legal and moral standing, at least in the field of public education.

The NAACP's task was at least less cumbersome than its opponents' task. The NAACP Legal Defense Fund had spearheaded all four lawsuits now included under *Brown v. Board of Education;* a few of the fund's lawyers had worked on two or more of the four cases. The NAACP's opponents were from four different states. Although the lawyers representing Topeka, Clarendon County, Delaware, and Prince Edward County informed each other of their plans, they essentially worked separately, each legal team preparing its own argument before the Supreme Court.

Ten days before the Supreme Court hearing, Marshall and his lawyers assembled at Howard University's law school to hold a mock trial. A group of law professors and lawyers played the role of the Supreme Court, and Marshall and his associates conducted a dress rehearsal of their presentation. The men acting as Supreme Court justices fired difficult questions at the NAACP's lawyers, prompting Marshall and his legal team to fine-tune their arguments and anticipate counterarguments. On December 9, Marshall and his lieutenants felt thoroughly prepared to present the most important case of their lives before the Supreme Court of the United States.

The Opening Salvo

The Supreme Court building in downtown Washington, D.C., is an imposing structure, a classical-style edifice calling to mind a magnificent temple of ancient Greece or Rome. The inner corridors are adorned with marble steps and columns, and the building's walls display panels and medallions depicting some of the great lawmakers of history—Solomon, Moses, Confucius, Muhammad, Charlemagne, and others. As Thurgood Marshall and his able assistants entered this magnificent building on December 9, 1952, perhaps they were encouraged by the motto inscribed in large letters above the entranceway: EQUAL JUSTICE UNDER LAW. For the next three days, they would try to persuade the justices of the Supreme Court that the United States should abide by that motto in the field of public education.

At about noon the nine black-robed justices of the Supreme Court entered the large courtroom and took their seats behind the dark mahogany bench that sits on an elevated platform at the head of the courtroom. After the justices were seated and the proceeding called to order, Robert Carter, the NAACP lawyer handling the Topeka case, approached the lectern positioned in front of the judges' bench and began to present his argument.

Carter began by charging that black students "have been denied equal protection of the law where the state requires segregated

The Supreme Court of the United States. The cases argued within these imposing walls have a tremendous impact on the course of American history.

schools. It denies them equal opportunities which the Fourteenth Amendment adequately secures." He added that segregation "severely handicaps Negro children in the pursuit of knowledge and makes it difficult for them to pursue their education." Midway through his presentation, however, the Supreme Court justices began peppering Carter with questions. Did not the *Gong Lum v. Rice* decision of 1927 allow the state of Mississippi to classify a Chinese girl as "colored" for the sake of placing her in a school for black children? Carter suggested that the *Gong Lum* decision merely allowed the state to classify someone as colored but not to deny anyone equal protection of the law. Justice Felix Frankfurter then asked Carter to confront the key issue directly: "Do we not have to face the fact that what you are challenging is something that was written into public law and adjudications of courts, including this Court, by a large body of decisions and, therefore, the question arises whether, and under what circumstances, this Court should now upset so long a course of decisions?" Carter responded by asserting, "I have no hesitancy in saying that the issue of 'separate but equal' should be faced . . . and should be squarely overruled."

After Carter completed his argument, his opposing lawyer, Paul Wilson, the assistant attorney general of Kansas, made only a short presentation before the Court. He stressed that the *Gong Lum* decision and others allowed states to classify citizens by race, and he disputed the NAACP's claim that segregated schools cause harm to black students.

Up next was Thurgood Marshall, appealing the *Briggs v. Elliott* decision. He sharply criticized the U.S. district court in Richmond for suggesting that segregation was a prerogative of the individual states, as the practice ran counter to the spirit of the Fourteenth Amendment. He cited several decisions in which the Supreme Court had prohibited the states from passing laws contrary to the Constitution. He shrewdly responded to the justices' questions. To one query on the Court's previous decisions on civil rights issues, Marshall replied, "I believe that there is a body of law that holds that distinctions on the basis of race are odious [hateful] and invidious [detestable]."

Marshall's opposing attorney was John W. Davis, one of the nation's top experts on constitutional law, a seventy-nine-year-old attorney from a prestigious New York law firm who had participated in more than 250 cases that were heard by the Supreme Court. On this day, the polished and experienced attorney gave a persuasive performance. The respectful justices of the Supreme Court interrupted Davis with questions only twice. He argued that South Carolina was on record with a commitment to improve its schools for black children. He recited the long line of precedents that allowed a state to classify citizens on the basis of race. He took issue with the findings of Kenneth Clark and other social scientists who maintained that segregation harmed black children. Davis concluded by stressing that "there is no reason assigned here why this Court or any other should reverse the findings of 90 years."

Arguments and Counterarguments

The next day, Spottswood Robinson, presenting the appeal in *Davis v. County School Board of Prince Edward County*, covered much of the same ground tread by Carter and Marshall in their arguments. His opponent, Justin Moore, legal counsel for the Prince Edward County school board, presented a devastating attack on the NAACP's position. Its key witness, Kenneth Clark, maintained Moore, was a man of warped judgments who had spent little time in the South and did not really know its people. The strike at Moton High, according to Moore, was not the result of student dissatisfaction with their educational facilities, but the result of outside agitators like the NAACP. He also asserted that the Fourteenth Amendment was not designed to govern local issues like public schooling.

In the Delaware case, the state's attorney general, Albert Young, spoke first because he was appealing the victory won by the NAACP in the lower court. Young argued that the district court had erred in its decision because the state was in the process of significantly improving its schools for black students. Jack Greenberg, arguing for the NAACP, countered Young's claim by pointing out to the Court that Delaware's plans for upgrading its schools for blacks were vague and indefinite; therefore, the lower court's order to open the whites-only schools to black students was justifiable and should be made permanent by order of the Supreme Court.

During this three-day ordeal, the Court also heard the *Bolling v. Sharpe* case, which was not included under the *Brown v. Board of Education* umbrella. On December 11, at about four o'clock in the afternoon, Thurgood Marshall and his tired team of attorneys left the trial room of the highest court in the United States anxious to return home to enjoy the holidays and await the Supreme Court's decision. It would be a long wait.

BOLLING V. SHARPE

In the spring of 1950, shortly after the NAACP's victories in the *Sweatt v. Painter* and *McLaurin v. Oklahoma* cases, a Washington, D.C., barber named Gardner Bishop approached Professor James Nabrit of the Howard University law school to ask him for help in his battle with the District of Columbia's school board. For three years Bishop had been battling the board over the condition of Browne Junior High, a school for Washington's black youngsters that his daughter attended. During the winter of 1947–1948, Bishop had led the students on a long strike to protest the school's inferior educational facilities. Bishop and his followers had filed a lawsuit, but their case, heard in the Washington, D.C., Court of Appeals in 1950 under the title *Carr v. Corning*, was lost. The appeals court had pronounced segregated schooling legal in the nation's capital.

Now, after the favorable rulings in the *Sweatt* and *McLaurin* cases, Bishop was ready to test the courts a second time. On September 11, 1950, the Washington barber accompanied eleven African American children to brand-new John Philip Sousa Junior High School and asked that the children be allowed to register. The students were turned away; the school was for white children only.

Early in 1951 James Nabrit filed a lawsuit in a district court on behalf of those eleven students, one of whom was named Spottswood Bolling, against C. Melvin Sharpe, president of Washington's board of education. The case, titled *Bolling v. Sharpe*, was heard in April.

Nabrit lost his case. The court ruled that the *Carr v. Corning* decision had clearly declared school segregation in the District of Columbia to be legal. Since Nabrit had targeted segregation itself, not the inferior conditions of Browne Junior High, as the focus of his lawsuit, the court offered no relief.

Nabrit intended to carry his case to the U.S. Court of Appeals, but while waiting for another turn in court, Nabrit was notified that the Supreme Court wished to hear his case on the same day that the *Brown v. Board of Education* case would be argued. *Bolling v. Sharpe* would not be included under the *Brown v. Board of Education* umbrella because it involved the District of Columbia, not one of the states. The Fourteenth Amendment specifically stated that no *state* could deprive citizens of the equal protection of the laws, but the amendment made no reference to the District of Columbia. Hence, *Bolling v. Sharpe* would have to be argued separately, and on somewhat different grounds.

But the Supreme Court's verdict in the Washington, D.C., case was the same as its verdict in *Brown v. Board of Education:* "In view of our decision that the Constitution prohibits the states from maintaining racially segregated public schools, it would be unthinkable that the same Constitution would impose a lesser duty on the Federal Government."

Thurgood Marshall (left), James Nabrit (center), and Jack Greenberg, three key figures in the fight against school segregation.

A Long Delay

The Supreme Court justices are always deliberate when they consider a case, especially when the case is as important as the one presented to them in December 1952. They review transcripts of the arguments, review the lower-court rulings, and pore over legal texts to search for relevant precedents. They also discuss the case among themselves before deciding on how to cast their individual votes. In the case of *Brown v. Board of Education*, the Supreme Court justices had not only to come to a decision on the constitutionality of segregated schools; they also had to decide whether their decision would affect only the schools and students cited in the lawsuits or the schools and students around the entire country. Moreover, if they cast out the practice of racially segregated schools, would they order those schools immediately closed, or would school boards be given a window of time to integrate their schools?

The Court wrestled with these issues during the opening months of 1953. Chief Justice Fred Vinson was leaning against the

---

 ## ARGUING BEFORE THE SUPREME COURT

Presenting a case before the Supreme Court is different from presenting a case before any other court. No witnesses are called to offer testimony, and the hearing lasts, at most, a few days, unlike criminal trials that can drag on for several months.

Before their appearance before the High Court, the lawyers for the competing parties submit legal briefs stating the key points of their arguments. Other parties are also free to submit briefs. For example, in the *Brown v. Board of Education* case, the U.S. attorney general, speaking for the federal government, filed a brief supporting the NAACP's position.

At the time of *Brown v. Board of Education*, arguments began at noon. At two o'clock, a thirty-minute lunch recess was called. Then the trial would resume for another two hours and adjourn precisely at 4:30 P.M.

The lawyer for the party appealing the lower-court ruling is allowed to address the Court first. That lawyer has one hour to present his or her client's case. Then the opposing lawyer has one hour to present his or her argument. During the last five minutes of the hour, the attorney is warned of the time by a white light implanted in the lectern. A red light flashes when the hour is up. The Court's justices are free to interrupt an attorney at any time. If an interruption takes place, the clock continues to tick, removing precious minutes from the attorney's presentation. If the lawyer does not use the allotted sixty minutes, he or she is allowed the unused time to offer a rebuttal of the opposing attorney's argument.

The process forces the lawyers to be direct and succinct, to render their arguments in clear and simple language. The attorneys must also possess the ability to respond quickly yet thoughtfully to a justice's question. Hence, the best Supreme Court hearings feature a fast-paced debate between individuals with finely tuned legal minds on crucial matters of constitutional law.

NAACP, as were Associate Justices Stanley Reed and Tom Clark. Associate Justices Hugo Black, William O. Douglas, Harold Burton, and Sherman Minton were siding with the NAACP. Justices Felix Frankfurter and Robert Jackson were undecided; they needed more time to consider the issue. On June 8, 1953, six months after the case was heard, Justice Frankfurter persuaded his colleagues on the Court to ask for a reargument later that year.

What troubled Frankfurter and the other justices was an issue that was mentioned but not thoroughly discussed when the case was argued in December: When Congress approved the Fourteenth Amendment back in 1868, did it intend the amendment to abolish segregation in public schools? The attorneys on both sides received from the Court a list of questions concerning that issue as well as several questions regarding how school desegregation could be effected, if indeed the Court felt compelled to outlaw Jim Crow schools. The reargument was set for October, then pushed back until December, a year after the first hearing.

Fred Vinson was among the justices who would hear Brown v. Board of Education. *Unfortunately, he did not live to see the end of the case; he suffered a fatal heart attack on September 8, 1953.*

On receiving the notice for reargument from the Supreme Court, the NAACP legal team went to work. Marshall and his cohorts spent the summer reviewing the congressional records for any references to public schools during the debates on the Fourteenth Amendment.

Their research proved relatively fruitless. The framers of the Fourteenth Amendment did not specifically consider the issue of public schooling. That was hardly surprising because public education was not widespread during the late 1860s. Many communities in the North had established tax-supported public schools; but the rural and war-ravished South was just beginning to establish free public schools, while the unsettled West had hardly begun to embark on the process toward free public education.

As the summer of 1953 ended, Thurgood Marshall decided upon a new approach to meet the Supreme Court's questions concerning the intent of the framers of the Fourteenth Amendment. Marshall and his associates would focus on the spirit of the discussion surrounding the enactment of the Fourteenth Amendment. The creators of that amendment, the NAACP would argue, wanted to erase racial inequality in the United States by guaranteeing every citizen equal protection under the law. Certainly any state-sponsored activity, such as public education, that did not offer all citizens equal protection and opportunity could be ruled unconstitutional, even if that activity was not specifically discussed during the debates over enactment of the Fourteenth Amendment.

Marshall and his colleagues began composing their legal brief along those lines. During the autumn of 1953, they vigorously wrote and revised. Their hard work resulted in a 235-page legal brief that argued that

> the very purpose of the Thirteenth, Fourteenth and Fifteenth Amendments was to effectuate a complete break with governmental action based on the established uses, customs and traditions of the slave era, to revolutionize the legal relationship between Negroes and whites, to destroy the inferior status of the Negro and place him upon a plane of complete equality with the white man.

Confident in this line of reasoning, Marshall and his colleagues were prepared for another day at the Supreme Court.

The Death of a Chief Justice

On September 8, 1953, while the NAACP attorneys were planning their strategy for the reargument of *Brown v. Board of Education*, Chief Justice Fred Vinson suffered a fatal heart attack in his Washington apartment. He was sixty-three years old. His death could not have been more untimely—just as the Supreme Court was deciding the most important case of the century.

To replace Vinson, President Dwight Eisenhower nominated Earl Warren, the popular and well-respected governor of California. Warren had a reputation for fairness and honesty. So widely was Warren admired that both the Republican and Democratic Parties nominated him for governor in the 1946 election. But to Thurgood Marshall and his associates, the new chief justice caused concerns. Would a brand-new chief justice take the radical step to outlaw school segregation and, hence, overthrow court decisions that had held authority for more than fifty years?

Furthermore, during World War II, Warren, as governor of California, spearheaded the effort to confiscate the property of Japanese Americans and force these citizens to live in detention camps until the end of the war. That policy had been enacted as a wartime measure by a governor fearful that Japanese American citizens would cause civil unrest while the United States was at war with Japan, but the NAACP attorneys reasoned that a governor unconcerned with the civil rights of Japanese American citizens might not be, by extension, sympathetic to the rights of African American citizens.

To prepare for the December reargument, Warren would review the entire testimony involving the four school desegregation cases. He would read the transcripts of the lower-court and Supreme Court hearings, study the legal briefs submitted by all parties, and discuss the case at length with his colleagues on the Court. On December 7, the new chief justice was prepared to hear the reargument for *Brown v. Board of Education*.

CHIEF JUSTICE EARL WARREN

When President Dwight Eisenhower nominated Governor Earl Warren of California as chief justice of the U.S. Supreme Court in September 1953, most legal experts predicted an era of conservatism in Supreme Court rulings. Warren, a conservative Republican, would certainly stress property rights and the rights of corporations. He was not expected to move the Court in any bold new directions.

Chief Justice Earl Warren replaced Fred Vinson on the Supreme Court. His nomination concerned Marshall and others, who were unsure whether Warren would be sympathetic to the desegregation cause.

Quite the opposite occurred. During Warren's sixteen years on the High Court, the rights of America's least powerful citizens received focused attention for the first time in American history. Warren seconded his opinion in the landmark school desegregation case of *Brown v. Board of Education of Topeka, Kansas*, with subsequent rulings that cast out segregation and promoted racial equality. In addition, the Warren Court decided several cases that enhanced the rights of those accused of crimes. In 1961, in the *Mapp v. Ohio* case, the Court ruled that illegally seized incriminating evidence could not be used to convict a person of a crime. In the *Gideon v. Wainwright* case of 1963, the Court negated a lower court's conviction of Clarence Gideon, a petty thief, because he had not been provided with a lawyer to represent him in his trial. In *Miranda v. Arizona*, decided in 1963, the Warren Court overturned a criminal conviction because the accused individual had not been informed of his constitutional right to remain silent and to speak with an attorney before being questioned by the police.

Some Americans thought that the Warren Court had gone too far in protecting the rights of criminals, making it harder for law enforcement officials to do their job. During the late 1960s, some American motorists displayed "Impeach Earl Warren" bumper stickers on their automobiles. Despite this criticism, constitutional scholars generally rate Warren as one of the two or three most influential chief justices in American history.

Warren retired from the Supreme Court in 1969. He died in 1974, at age eighty-three.

The Reargument

At one o'clock in the morning on December 7, 1953, a seventy-six-year-old black man took his place in line outside the Supreme Court building to wait to be admitted to the visitors' gallery in the Supreme Court trial room. By dawn, a line of people had formed down the block vying to be spectators. When the Court opened, they filed in and took their seats, ready to witness the case that, by this time, had captured the entire nation's attention.

At one o'clock in the afternoon, Spottswood Robinson approached the lectern, faced the justices, and began outlining the NAACP's argument. He emphasized that the Fourteenth Amendment must be broadly interpreted as an effort to end all forms of racial discrimination. Thurgood Marshall, following Robinson, flatly asserted that the Supreme Court had ruled incorrectly in the *Plessy v. Ferguson* and *Gong Lum v. Rice* cases by allowing states to segregate citizens by race. When it was his turn, their opposing lawyer, John W. Davis, refuted Marshall's point by identifying seven specific cases in which the Supreme Court had given its support to the "separate but equal" doctrine. He also pointed out the logistical problems of ending school segregation and asked the justices whether Clarendon County's black students would be much better off if they had three or four white children in their class. He ended his argument by asserting that the Supreme Court "cannot sit as a glorified board of education for the state of South Carolina or any other state." Davis's argument was fortified by the Virginia attorney general J. Lindsay Almond, who defended segregated schooling with a flourish, declaring that "with the help and the sympathy and the love and respect of the white people of the South, the colored man has risen under that educational process to a place of eminence and respect throughout the nation. It has served him well."

The next day Marshall was again at the lectern, offering a rebuttal to the remarks of his opposing attorneys. According to Marshall, their only defense of segregated education was "(1) that they got together and decided it is best for the races to be separated and (2) that it has existed for over a century." Marshall shrewdly demolished both arguments, then added an informal comment that appealed to the justices' hearts rather than to their finely tuned legal minds:

> I got the feeling on hearing the discussion yesterday that when you put a white child in a school with a whole lot of colored children, the child would fall apart or something. Everybody knows that is not true.

> Those same kids in Virginia and South Carolina—and I have seen them do it—they play in the streets together, they play on their farms together, they go down the road together, they separate to go to school, they come out of school and play ball together. They have to be separated in school.

On the third day of the hearing, the Delaware and *Bolling v. Sharpe* cases were reheard. The attorneys for each side rehashed many of the points made on the previous two days, with James

Marshall's persuasive arguments before the Supreme Court helped turn Brown v. Board of Education *in his favor.*

Nabrit, the NAACP lawyer handling the *Bolling* case, offering the most eloquent verbal flourish of the proceeding. "Our Constitution has no provision across it that all men are equal but that white men are more equal than others," he declared. "Under this statute and under this country, under this Constitution, and under the protections of this Court, we believe that we, too, are equal."

The reargument ended just before three o'clock in the afternoon on December 9. Again the NAACP's lawyers left the courtroom exhausted, but anxious to hear the results of the Court's deliberations.

The Court Renders Its Decision

After the reargument, the justices of the Supreme Court repeated the process that they had performed exactly a year earlier. They reviewed transcripts of the hearings, reread the legal briefs presented by all parties, combed through legal texts to find relevant precedent cases, and discussed the case for hours among themselves, at both formal meetings and informal lunches.

The NAACP's lawyers had won over a majority of the justices during the reargument. By late February 1954, Chief Justice Warren had determined that at least seven justices favored delivering an opinion that outlawed segregated public schools. But Warren wanted no dissenting opinions offered on this important case; he wanted the Court to speak with a single voice. By March only Justice Stanley Reed—a Southerner, a Kentucky man—sided against the NAACP. Warren began to write his opinion, still trying to persuade Reed to join his fellow justices in a unanimous decision. By early May Reed had been persuaded to support Warren's carefully composed opinion. Warren had a unanimous Court.

On May 17, 1954, the justices of the Supreme Court assembled to deliver a handful of opinions in cases recently decided. The Court generally gives no advance notice of which rulings will be announced on any given day. Newspaper reporters assemble in the Supreme Court's press room and receive copies of the opinions handed down and then go off to write their articles for their newspapers. At about 12:45 P.M., Banning Whittington, the

Supreme Court's press secretary, entered the press room and announced that the chief justice would momentarily be reading the Court's decision in the school desegregation cases. Immediately, reporters began grabbing their briefcases, pulling out notepads, and dashing upstairs to the trial room. History was about to be made.

Several minutes before one o'clock, Chief Justice Warren announced that he was ready to read the Court's opinion in the case of *Brown v. Board of Education of Topeka, Kansas*. With reporters poised with their pencils and spectators riveted in attention, Warren began to read his opinion. First, he reviewed the facts of the case—the plaintiffs' claims, the decisions of the lower courts, the points presented at argument and reargument, the relevant precedent cases. Warren read for several minutes without hinting at the Court's decision. Then Warren began to address the key issue: Did the framers of the Fourteenth Amendment intend it to cover public education? "In approaching this problem," explained Warren, "we cannot turn the clock back to 1868 when the Amendment was adopted, or even to 1896 when *Plessy v. Ferguson* was written. We must consider public education in the light of its full development and present place in American life throughout the Nation."

Warren went on to explain the importance of public education in American life:

> It is required in the performance of our most basic public responsibilities, even service in the armed forces. It is the very foundation of good citizenship. Today it is a principal instrument in awakening the child to cultural values, in preparing him for later professional training, and in helping him adjust normally to his environment.

Then Warren addressed the question that the entire nation was waiting for the Court to answer: "Does segregation of children in public schools solely on the basis of race, even though the physical facilities and other 'tangible' factors may be equal, deprive the children of the minority group of equal education opportunities? We believe that it does."

Under the leadership of Chief Justice Earl Warren (front row, center), the U.S. Supreme Court promoted school desegregation with its landmark decision in Brown v. Board of Education.

Warren went on to defend the Court's decision in simple yet eloquent terms. Acknowledging the research of Kenneth Clark and others, Warren asserted that segregated schools damage black students by generating "a feeling of inferiority as to their status in the community that may affect their hearts and minds in a way unlikely ever to be undone." He continued:

> We conclude that in the field of public education the doctrine of "separate but equal" has no place. Separate educational facilities are inherently unequal. Therefore, we hold that the plaintiffs and others similarly situated . . . are . . . deprived of the equal protection of the laws guaranteed by the Fourteenth Amendment.

Warren concluded by acknowledging the difficulty of immediately implementing the Court's decision. He asked that both parties submit legal briefs regarding implementation six months hence. Then Warren delivered the Court's opinion in the case of *Bolling v. Sharpe.* In light of the Court's decision in *Brown v.*

Board of Education, the decision in the Washington, D.C., case was not surprising: "We hold that racial segregation in the public schools of the District of Columbia is a denial of the due process of law guaranteed by the Fifth Amendment to the Constitution."

The Reaction

Marshall and his exhausted assistants were ecstatic. "I was so happy I was numb," Marshall later said. Most on his legal team were black men who had grown up under Jim Crow conditions. Several had been denied entry to the nation's elite law schools because of their race. They had taken their complaint—and the complaints of millions of African American children—to the Supreme Court, and the chief justice had essentially told them, Yes, you are equal before the laws of this country; segregation, at least in public education, is against the law.

Predictably, reaction around the United States was mixed. Dean Erwin Griswold of the Harvard University law school declared that the Supreme Court, "in clear and simple language, has given an interpretation of the rather plain meaning of the 'equal protection' clause of the Constitution." An editorial in the *New York Times* asserted that the Court "squared the country's basic law with its conscience and deepest convictions." The *Des Moines Register* concurred, editorializing that the Court "has begun the erasure of one of American democracy's blackest marks with its ruling that racial segregation in public schools is unconstitutional."

From the South, however, came voices filled with anger. According to Herman Talmadge, governor of Georgia, "The United States Supreme Court by its decision has reduced the Constitution to a mere scrap of paper." The *Charleston News & Courier* claimed that the Court's decision "drove another nail into the coffin of states." But other Southerners reacted calmly and reasonably to the Court's decree. "What is needed most in all the states affected is a calm, rational approach. Panic and the losing of tempers will cause more harm than good," the *Atlanta Constitution* editorialized. The editors of the *Birmingham News*

Public reaction to the Brown v. Board of Education *ruling was mixed. Herman Talmadge, governor of Georgia, was among the faction outraged by the Court's decision.*

agreed, calling for "analysis and solution in a calm, orderly fashion." Senator Russell B. Long of Louisiana questioned the Court's decision but offered sensible advice to his fellow Southerners: "My oath of office requires me to accept it as the law. Every citizen is likewise bound by this oath of allegiance to his country. I urge all Southern officials to avoid any sort of rash or hasty action."

Implementation of the Court's order would not be hasty. The NAACP urged the Court to order immediate implementation of its decree to desegregate schools. The Court studied the issue intensely. On May 31, 1955, one year and two weeks after the *Brown* decision was announced, the Supreme Court delivered an enforcement decree, sometimes referred to as *Brown v. Board of Education II.* The Court acknowledged the difficulty of desegregating schools immediately. Local courts would be responsible for enforcing the Supreme Court's ruling, though those courts "may find that additional time is necessary to carry out the ruling in an effective manner." The Court's decree concluded by urging school districts to admit students on a nondiscriminatory basis "with all deliberate speed." School desegregation was underway, but fully integrating America's public schools would take many years.

Chapter 5

The Birth of the Civil Rights Movement

SOME SCHOOL BOARDS in the South began plans for integration immediately after the Supreme Court's desegregation order in May 1954. Baltimore, Louisville, and Washington, D.C., began the process for the new 1954–1955 school year. In other areas, movement was painfully slow, and the integration process would take more than a decade.

Ironically, the Supreme Court decision on school desegregation would have a more profound and immediate effect outside the classroom. A year after the *Brown v. Board of Education* decision, a U.S. district court ruled that the city of Baltimore could no longer segregate its bathing beaches or public parks and recreational facilities. Later in 1955 the Supreme Court ruled that the city of Atlanta could not continue to exclude blacks from public golf courses. Chief Justice Earl Warren's eloquent condemnation of segregated public schools was received as a general indictment of all forms of government-sponsored segregation. Suddenly, African American civil rights leaders had a legal precedent with which to attack segregation of all kinds. In a 1957 speech, a fresh young civil rights leader from the South named Martin Luther King Jr. articulated the importance of the Supreme Court's 1954 decision in launching his battle against racial segregation:

> In this decision the Supreme Court of this nation unanimously affirmed that the old Plessy doctrine must go.

This decision came as a legal and sociological death blow to an evil that had occupied the throne of American life for several decades. It affirmed in no uncertain terms that separate facilities are inherently unequal and that to segregate a child because of his race is to deny him equal protection of the law. With the coming of this great decision we could gradually see the old order of segregation and discrimination passing away, and the new order of freedom and justice coming into being.

The ten years following the Court's decision saw the birth and development of a civil rights movement unprecedented in U.S. history, as Americans, both black and white, struggled to implement the Court's belief that racial segregation ran counter to the principles put forth in the Constitution.

The Montgomery Bus Boycott

Nowhere was the impact of the Supreme Court's 1954 decision shown more poignantly than in Montgomery, Alabama. On December 1, 1955, a forty-three-year-old Montgomery seamstress named Rosa Parks broke a city ordinance that required black passengers to forfeit their seats on municipal buses so that white passengers could sit. When Parks refused to surrender her seat to a white passenger who boarded the filled bus, the driver reported her to the police. She was fined $14 for her offense. Parks, who served as secretary in the local chapter of the NAACP, made her situation known to her chapter president, who called a meeting of Montgomery's African American community leaders. Among them were several clergymen, including Martin Luther King Jr. The group called itself the Montgomery Improvement Association (MIA) and elected the twenty-six-year-old King as its president. It immediately called upon all of Montgomery's black citizens to boycott the city's municipal buses.

A bus boycott would cause Montgomery's black citizens difficulties. Few could afford to own cars, so most used the buses to get to work. But on Monday, December 5, the first day of the boycott, more than 90 percent of Montgomery's black citizens

Rosa Parks is fingerprinted after being arrested. Parks made history in December 1955 when she refused to forfeit her bus seat to a white passenger, triggering the Montgomery bus boycott.

who routinely rode the buses boycotted them. They walked to work. They rode bicycles. They formed carpools. Black taxicab drivers drove black people to work for the cost of bus fare. Most white citizens of Montgomery expected the boycott to last a day or two, but at the start of the second week, it was still going strong. An elderly woman who was walking a long distance to get to work said, "My feet is tired, but my soul is rested."

King and MIA leaders met with Montgomery's mayor W. A. Gayle to express their concerns. They wanted an immediate end to segregated seating aboard Montgomery's buses; otherwise, the boycott would continue. Mayor Gayle refused; he did not take the boycott seriously. But he did not realize how the spirit in the black community had changed since 1954. The Supreme Court had stated that segregation violated the Constitution. Montgomery's citizens felt that they had the force of the law on their side.

REVEREND MARTIN LUTHER KING JR.

The greatest leader to emerge from the Civil Rights movement was not a lawyer but a clergyman. A native of Atlanta, Martin Luther King Jr., whose father and grandfather were also ministers, graduated first in his class at Crozer Theological Seminary in Pennsylvania, attended Boston University, and, in 1954, returned to the South to assume the post of pastor at Dexter Avenue Baptist Church in Montgomery, Alabama. (A year later, he completed his doctoral degree in theology at Boston University.)

King was not content to play the role of the traditional clergyman who exhorted his flock to avoid sin and lead good lives so that they may achieve happiness in the afterlife. He began to involve himself in the political and social problems that Montgomery's black citizens faced in the era of Jim Crow. In 1955 he was named president of the Montgomery Improvement Association, which led the boycott that ended segregated seating on Montgomery's municipal buses.

In 1957 King, determined to expand his battle for racial equality beyond Montgomery's borders, founded the Southern Christian Leadership Conference (SCLC), whose mission was to fight all forms of racial segregation in the United States. Two years later King left Dexter Avenue Baptist Church to work full-time for SCLC. During the next decade King traveled throughout the United States waging a campaign to end racial injustice. With stirring speeches and nonviolent protests, he alerted the nation to the plight of its black citizens. In 1963 he delivered his famous "I Have a Dream" speech before three hundred thousand protesters who had embarked on the March on Washington for Jobs and Freedom. That same year King, writing from a jail cell in Birmingham, Alabama, articulated his political philosophy in a moving essay titled "Letter from a Birmingham Jail." He spearheaded protest marches throughout the South, demanding on behalf of black Americans the right to vote, opportunities for quality education and good jobs, and an end to all forms of segregation.

On April 4, 1968, the day after delivering a speech on behalf of striking sanitation workers in Memphis, Tennessee, King was killed by an assassin. His untimely death cut short a career devoted to the cause of racial equality. Encouraged by King's leadership, African Americans had, from 1955 through 1968, purged from the United States almost all of the most blatant and overt forms of racial injustice and segregation.

The boycott started to hurt Montgomery's white citizens. Downtown shopkeepers began to complain that black people were not patronizing their shops because the shoppers would not travel on buses. The bus company was losing almost two-thirds of its income.

Martin Luther King Jr. was a strong voice in the fight for civil rights. His eloquent speeches and nonviolent protests incited Americans to oppose racial inequities.

Still, the mayor denounced the boycott and refused to listen to the MIA's appeals.

In January King's house was bombed, but the boycott continued. In February King and several MIA leaders were arrested for breaking a local law that prohibited boycotts. King was fined $500 (a conviction later overruled by a higher court). The boycott continued. The MIA attempted to get relief in the courts; and in June a federal district court, bowing to the precedent set in *Brown v. Board of Education*, ruled that Montgomery's Jim Crow bus law violated the Fourteenth Amendment of the Constitution. The city appealed the decision, so the boycott continued.

It lasted 381 days. On December 20, 1956, city officials received an order from the Supreme Court to end all segregation practices on its municipal buses. On hearing the news, one boycotter cried out, "God Almighty has spoken from Washington, D.C.!" The next morning King boarded a Montgomery bus, took a seat in the front row, and rode crosstown. "We are glad to have you this morning," the driver said.

Encouraged by his victory in Alabama, King broadened his battle to end racial segregation to eventually include the entire South. Racial barriers began falling across the entire region—at public beaches, at sports arenas and golf courses, on trains and buses. The idea of segregation, defended by law and accepted by custom before 1954, was quickly losing its standing on American soil. To many Americans, the notion had become distasteful. The Supreme Court's decision of 1954 had not only deprived segregation of its legal force; it had rendered segregation morally repugnant as well.

The Little Rock Crisis

Though racial barriers across the country were falling, school integration moved along at a slow pace. Few schools across the South integrated immediately; for those that did, the process was often painful. Nowhere was it more difficult than at Central High School in Little Rock, Arkansas.

After the Supreme Court's 1954 desegregation ruling was announced, the Little Rock school board made known its intention to comply with the Court's decree as soon as possible. Eighty percent of the city's citizens were white, however, and many did not like the idea of black students mixing with white students in public schools. Integration plans stalled. Finally, the school board announced that nine African American students would be allowed to attend all-white Central High School at the start of the 1957–1958 school year. Immediately, Arkansas governor Orval Faubus objected, announcing that he would not "be a party to any attempt to force acceptance of change to which the people are so overwhelmingly opposed." To back his words, Governor Faubus ordered the Arkansas National Guard to surround Central High School on the opening day of classes so that the nine black students could not enter the building. White students gathered outside the school building and taunted the black students as they approached the school.

President Dwight Eisenhower summoned Governor Faubus to Newport, Rhode Island, where the president was vacationing, to discuss the situation. The president convinced Governor Faubus to withdraw the guardsmen and allow the black students, now called the Little Rock Nine, to begin attending classes. When the Little Rock Nine entered Central High School the next day, a large and unruly mob had formed around the building. The black students were insulted and threatened. The beleaguered students returned home, refusing to attend school unless their safety was insured.

President Eisenhower sensed the seriousness of the situation in Little Rock. In a radio address, he implored Little Rock's citizens to accept the Supreme Court's orders and allow for the peaceful integration of Central High School. On September 24, the president dispatched one thousand troops from the 101st Airborne Division to Little Rock and placed under their command another ten thousand Arkansas National Guardsmen. The next day soldiers armed with rifles and fixed bayonets arrived at Central High School to contend with the mob of protesters that was expected to form. A battalion of troopers met the Little Rock Nine at the home of one of the black students to escort them to school. Protected by federal troops, the nine black students entered the building and began attending class. For the next two months, troopers were on hand to ensure the students' safety and quell any uprising of Little Rock citizens who wished to obstruct the Court's order to desegregate public schools.

Although some of Central High's white students reasonably accepted integration, the Little Rock Nine did not have an easy time at Central High School. Early in the school year, Jane Emery, editor of the school paper, urged her fellow students to rise to the challenge of integration. "This is the opportunity for you as citizens of Arkansas and students of Little Rock Central High to

Even after school segregation became illegal, overt racism prevented peaceful integration. Here, federal troops at Central High School in Little Rock, Arkansas, insure the safety of the school's first black students.

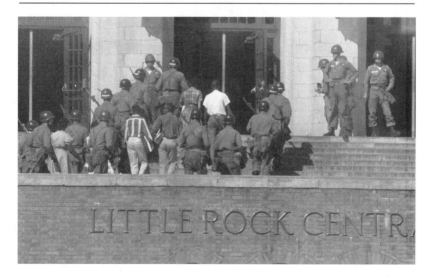

show the world that Arkansas is a progressive, thriving state of wide-awake alert people," Emery advised in an editorial. When Ralph Brodie, president of Central High's student body, was asked by a reporter how he felt about integration, he sensibly replied, "If it's a court order, we have to follow it and abide by the law." Robin Woods, a member of the student council, accepted the change at his school calmly. "That was the first time I'd ever gone to school with a Negro," he told a reporter after the Little Rock Nine's first day of class, "and it didn't hurt a bit."

Other students were far less sympathetic. In the middle of the school year, Minniejean Brown, one of the Little Rock Nine, told a reporter, "They throw rocks, they spill ink on your clothes, they call you 'nigger,' they just keep bothering you every five minutes. The white students hate me." Brown was expelled for

Elizabeth Eckford, one of the first black students to attend classes at Central High School, maintains a dignified posture while white students shout racial epithets.

JAMES MEREDITH INTEGRATES OLE MISS

One of the most memorable school integration battles was waged at the University of Mississippi in 1962. On May 31, 1961, James Meredith, a black resident of Mississippi and an air force veteran, applied for admission to the University of Mississippi, a 114-year-old institution that had never enrolled a black student. Meredith's application was turned down.

Meredith filed a lawsuit, but his appeal was rejected by a federal district court judge. In June 1962, however, a U.S. court of appeals, bowing to the precedent established by *Brown v. Board of Education*, ruled that Meredith's rejection was based solely on his race and, hence, ordered Meredith admitted to the University of Mississippi (affectionately called "Ole Miss").

In September, when Meredith tried to register for classes, however, Ole Miss officials again turned him away. In a televised speech, Mississippi governor Ross Barnett declared, "No school will be integrated in Mississippi while I'm the governor." On September 24 the appeals court that had ordered Meredith admitted again told Ole Miss officials to allow Meredith to register. Again the university refused. The court informed Barnett that if he did not comply with its order, he would be found in contempt of court, arrested, and fined $10,000 per day.

Barnett refused to act until Attorney General Robert Kennedy notified him that the federal government was determined to see Meredith enroll at Ole Miss. Under this kind of pressure, Barnett relented and allowed Meredith to register on Sunday, September 30. Kennedy dispatched three hundred armed federal marshals to accompany Meredith to the registrar's office in case violence broke out.

When Meredith arrived on campus to register, a crowd of twenty-five hundred Ole Miss students and other protesters were there to block his entrance. The unruly crowd threw bricks and bottles at federal marshals, who retaliated by spraying the crowd with tear gas. Several of the agitators fired weapons, wounding a marshal and killing two bystanders—a journalist and a jukebox repairman.

The next day, the president federalized five thousand Mississippi National Guardsmen and ordered them to protect Meredith and keep peace on campus and in the university town of Oxford. On Monday morning, October 1, Meredith registered for classes and began his matriculation at the University of Mississippi. Though he was often the target of insults and threats, Meredith completed his course work and graduated on August 18, 1963. He later enrolled at the Columbia University School of Law and became active in civil rights causes. In 1966 he was wounded by a gunshot from a sniper while participating in a voter registration march from Tennessee to Mississippi.

calling a fellow student "white trash" after the white student had called her a "nigger bitch." Ernest Green, who on May 29, 1958, became the first of the Little Rock Nine to graduate from Central High School, said that almost every day someone called him a "nigger." The students and their parents received threats throughout the school year.

When the school year ended, the Little Rock school board again tried to evade the Supreme Court's desegregation order. The board convinced a district court in Arkansas to approve a measure that would suspend integration at Little Rock's public schools for another two and a half years. The NAACP immediately appealed the district court's ruling to the Supreme Court. The appeal was heard under the title of *Cooper v. Aaron* in August. A month later, the Court unanimously nullified the lower court's order. Chief Justice Warren informed the school board of Little Rock that the Supreme Court's decision in the *Brown v. Board of Education* case can "neither be nullified openly or directly . . . nor nullified indirectly . . . through evasive schemes for segregation."

The school board, with Governor Faubus's assistance, continued its effort to evade the Supreme Court's order. Governor Faubus masterminded a scheme to close Little Rock's public schools and turn them into private institutions. For the 1958–1959 school year, Little Rock's public schools remained closed. White students attended private schools or paid to attend schools in other cities. The black students who had been allowed to integrate returned to black schools.

In June 1959, a U.S. district court voided Governor Faubus's scheme, calling it unconstitutional and ordering Little Rock's public schools reopened on a nonsegregated basis. The following September, several black students enrolled in Central High School with little ado. The Supreme Court's 1954 decision was finally obeyed in Little Rock, Arkansas.

Other Desegregation Efforts

The Supreme Court had clearly launched a desegregation order that did not stop at the schoolhouse door. In the late 1950s and early 1960s, desegregationists across the United States worked

Students at Little Rock Junior High School protest the admission of black students. The integration of Little Rock's schools was met with resistance from the public, the school board, and the governor.

tirelessly to cast out all remaining evidence of the Jim Crow era. In 1954 the Court had outlawed segregation only in public schools. Subsequent rulings by the Supreme Court and lower courts, however, invalidated segregation in public places financed by tax dollars—parks, golf courses, beaches. The next battlegrounds for the opponents of segregation were in privately owned public places, such as apartment buildings, restaurants, motels, and amusement parks. Martin Luther King and his followers reasoned that if segregation was considered unlawful and immoral in government-financed public places, it should be eliminated in privately owned public places as well.

The first battleground in this new desegregation effort became restaurants and lunch counters. Throughout the South, blacks were not allowed to sit and be served at certain eating places. On February 1, 1960, four African American students from North Carolina Agricultural and Technical College entered a Woolworth's five-and-ten store, sat at the whites-only lunch counter, and asked to be served. The waitress refused to serve the students, who remained seated until the store closed. The next day they returned with twenty additional students, with the same result: no service. The third day a larger group of black students, as well as several white students, occupied all but three of the sixty-three seats in the Woolworth's luncheonette area. Inspired by what was happening in Greensboro, black and white students all over North Carolina and Virginia began similar sit-ins in public eateries that did not serve black patrons. Martin Luther King applauded the students, asserting that they had earned "honored places in the world-wide struggle for freedom."

The movement spread throughout the South during the summer of 1960, but the fight to end segregated eating places was not easy. In Jackson, Mississippi, white hecklers poured drinks and ketchup on the protesters, who sat at perfect attention in a gesture of nonviolent protest. In Nashville, Tennessee, eighty-one protesters who sat passively in a restaurant were

Students defy racism during a sit-in at a Jackson, Mississippi, lunch counter. The intolerant crowd showered the protesters with mustard, ketchup, and sugar while they sat peacefully at the counter.

arrested for disorderly conduct. In some places, local police dragged out the protesters and beat them with billy clubs. Martin Luther King was arrested during a restaurant luncheonette sit-in in Atlanta. Charges were dropped only after Senator John Kennedy, the Democratic Party's candidate for president in the upcoming election, appealed to a local judge.

But the sit-ins were working. In May several stores in Nashville that were losing business because of the protests desegregated their lunch counters. Hot Shoppes, a national chain of luncheonettes, desegregated in June. Other chains followed suit, some because the sit-ins had severely disrupted business; some because they saw the opportunity to attract black patrons; some because they realized that segregation was part of a social order whose time had come and gone. Eventually, in 1964, a new Civil Rights Act would prohibit discrimination of any "restaurant, cafeteria, lunch room, lunch counter, soda fountain, or other facility principally engaged in selling food for consumption on the premises."

Freedom Riders

The year after the sit-in movement, a newly formed civil rights organization titled the Congress of Racial Equality (CORE) called for volunteers to launch an attack on segregated bus stations and terminals throughout the South. On May 4 thirteen CORE volunteers boarded a Greyhound bus in Washington, D.C., that was headed for Alabama and Louisiana. They planned to reach New Orleans on May 17, the seventh anniversary of the Supreme Court's decision in the *Brown* case. Along the way, these "Freedom Riders" intended to integrate whites-only washrooms, drink from whites-only water fountains, and flout other Jim Crow laws still in effect in Southern bus terminals.

When the bus reached a terminal in Anniston, Alabama, it was attacked by an angry mob of whites. The bus windows were broken, and its tires were slashed. Repairs were made, and the bus moved on, but it was attacked again and burned several miles outside Anniston. A CORE group on another bus was

A WAVE OF CIVIL RIGHTS LEGISLATION

In the wake of the *Brown v. Board of Education* decision came a demand for federal legislation to promote racial equality in the United States. In 1954 the Supreme Court acted to end segregation in public schools. During the next ten years, the Congress and presidents created landmark civil rights legislation designed to eliminate racial discrimination in all areas of American life.

The Civil Rights Act of 1957, the first since 1875, established a special civil rights division within the Justice Department to handle offenses concerning civil rights. The bill, passed by Congress and signed into law by President Dwight Eisenhower during the summer of 1957, also mandated strong penalties for interfering with any citizen's right to vote. Congress acted again in 1960 to ensure the voting rights of African American citizens by allowing courts to appoint voting referees in any district where citizens had been prevented from voting due to their race. The Civil Rights Act of 1960 also contained language stipulating penalties for anyone carrying explosives that would be used to damage homes, churches, or schools—a measure designed to punish those who had bombed or threatened to bomb the homes and churches of civil rights leaders like Martin Luther King.

Perhaps the most sweeping piece of legislation to result from the Civil Rights movement was the Civil Rights Act of 1964. Pushed through Congress by President Lyndon Johnson, a Southerner, the bill prohibited discrimination in stores, restaurants, hotels and inns, theaters, sports arenas, and other public places. Thus, restaurants could no longer refuse to serve black patrons, theaters and sports arenas could not force black customers to sit in special sections, and hotels and other lodging places could no longer close their doors to black travelers. The law tried to put an end to all Jim Crow practices everywhere in the United States.

The following year Congress again acted decisively in the area of civil rights by enacting the Voting Rights Act. The act, passed after a stunning protest march from Selma to Montgomery, Alabama, involving hundreds of protesters clamoring for the right to register and vote, attempted to wipe out any barriers that prevented African American citizens from exercising their right to use the ballot box.

---

beaten by white protesters at a terminal in Birmingham, Alabama. The CORE protesters eventually reached New Orleans by airplane. Another group of Freedom Riders en route from Nashville to Birmingham was met at their point of destination by a mob of white protesters who physically beat the Freedom Riders without interference from local police.

Freedom Riders were often verbally assaulted and suffered physical attacks at the hands of angry white mobs. Here, Freedom Riders survey the remains of their bus, burned beyond repair by white protesters.

During the summer of 1961, scores of Freedom Riders rode buses to the terminal in Jackson, Mississippi, merely to use the whites-only rest rooms. Many were arrested and given thirty- or sixty-day jail sentences. Finally, in September, under pressure from President Kennedy and Attorney General Robert Kennedy, the Interstate Commerce Commission issued an order banning segregation of any kind in terminals that accommodated interstate travelers. Hence, another barrier separating the races in the United States came down.

In a speech delivered in April 1960, Martin Luther King, encouraged by the widespread war against segregation being waged throughout the South, boldly declared, "Segregation is on its death bed now, and the only uncertain thing is about when it will be buried." This wave of civil rights initiatives that began in the mid-1950s and extended into the 1960s became known as the Civil Rights movement. Surely, the movement had its roots in earlier decades—in Thurgood Marshall's courtroom victories during the 1930s and 1940s, in Jackie Robinson's integration of major league baseball diamonds in 1947—but the Supreme Court's 1954 decision in the case of *Brown v. Board of Education* had given the movement both the legal standing and moral force that it needed to flourish and succeed.

Epilogue

The Legacy of *Brown v. Board of Education*

THE U.S. SUPREME COURT'S decision in the *Brown v. Board of Education* case triggered great changes in American society. Chief Justice Earl Warren's eloquently written opinion deprived racial segregation of its moral force, prompting the razing of racial barriers everywhere in American life and extending the rights and freedoms itemized in the Constitution to all Americans, regardless of race. But did the High Court's 1954 decision really end racial segregation in America's public schools? And if Warren's words did effectively promote racial integration in the nation's public schools, did African American students profit educationally from that development? More than forty years after the *Brown v. Board of Education* case was settled, the answers to those questions are not yet completely clear.

Desegregation Versus Integration

In its 1955 implementation decree, sometimes referred to as *Brown v. Board of Education II*, the Supreme Court urged public school boards throughout the United States to proceed with plans for desegregation "with all deliberate speed." Actual compliance with the Court's order emphasized the "deliberate" rather than the "speed." In 1964 only 1 percent of black children living in the South attended schools with white children, suggesting that the High Court's order was essentially being ignored. During the next several years, however, as lower courts began to compel local school boards to desegregate the schools in their districts, the desegregation process proceeded more rapidly. By 1972 almost half of the South's black elementary and high school students attended schools with white pupils.

During that time period, however, a different phenomenon was occurring in the North, where school segregation had not generally been promoted by the force of law. During the 1960s the changes wrought by the Civil Rights movement often resulted in increased tensions between whites and blacks. These tensions exploded into full-scale race riots in several cities outside the South throughout the decade—most tragically in Watts, California, in 1965; in Newark, New Jersey, in 1967; and in Detroit, Michigan, in 1967. The racial tensions in the North's urban centers prompted many white families to leave the inner cities and take up residence in the suburbs. This exodus of white citizens from the North's big cities, sometimes called "white flight," left many inner cities with nearly all-black populations. Hence, the public schools in these communities

This photo, taken shortly after the monumental Brown v. Board of Education *case, belies the racial status of public schools during this era. Most schools ignored the Court's order to desegregate.*

became, like the earlier Jim Crow schools of the South, almost entirely black. So the desegregation of public schools that was taking place in the South during the late 1960s and 1970s was offset by the phenomenon known as "white flight." Northern schools gradually became segregated institutions, not because of laws that mandated segregation but because the population in many inner-city school districts included so few white citizens. Hence, a new kind of segregation, prompted by people's relocation patterns rather than by law, came into existence.

DeWitt Clinton High School in Bronx, New York, perfectly illustrates how segregation took root in Northern inner-city schools. During the 1930s and 1940s, the school served Italian and Jewish neighborhoods in the Bronx as well as black and Latino neighborhoods in Harlem. Hence, the school's student body was richly mixed. By the late 1960s, most of the Bronx's white families had moved to the suburbs of Long Island, New Jersey, or southern Connecticut, and DeWitt Clinton High School was left with a student population almost entirely black and Latino. Because of the moving patterns of the Bronx population, it had become, in a sense, a segregated school.

The Supreme Court had clearly outlawed legally mandated *segregation*. School boards could no longer make students of one race attend one school and students of another race attend a different school. But could the Court mandate *integration?* Could the Supreme Court and lower courts force school boards in all-white suburbs to enroll black students? Could the courts compel school boards in essentially black inner cities to enroll a representative group of white students to achieve the goal of educational integration? The Supreme Court would tackle that issue in several cases that came before it in the late 1960s and 1970s.

Busing

In 1968 a federal district court in Virginia ruled that the school board of New Kent County had not moved decisively enough to end racial segregation in its public schools. New Kent County had employed an open-enrollment system that allowed students to attend schools of their choice. But most black students still opted to attend all-black schools, and the handful of black students who chose to attend mostly white schools were too often subject to ridicule and other forms of harassment. In the case titled *Green v. County School Board of Kent County, Virginia*, the Supreme Court unanimously upheld the district court's ruling that the school board must make a more substantial effort to integrate its schools. The Court suggested that schools should have a student population that mirrored the population of the surrounding area. In other words, if a county's population is 75 percent white and 25 percent black, each school in that county should have a student body that was approximately 75 percent white and 25 percent black. Thus, the High Court tried to promote integration rather than merely ending segregation. The Court's decision in the *Green v. County School Board* case was the last under the directorship of Earl Warren. He retired in 1969, and Warren Burger was named the new chief justice.

A year after the *Green v. County School Board* decision, the Supreme Court, in a case titled *Alexander v. Holmes County Board of Education*, again acted to promote school integration. The board of education of Holmes County in Mississippi had asked for a delay in implementing school desegregation. A lower court favored the delay, but the Supreme Court asserted that the notion of "deliberate speed" was no longer operative fifteen years after the first *Brown v. Board of Education* decision: "Under explicit holdings of this Court, the obligation of every school district is to terminate dual school systems at once and to operate now and hereafter only unitary schools."

In 1971 the Court made its most forceful effort to try to integrate America's public schools. A year earlier a federal district court had ordered that the schools of Charlotte, North Carolina, and surrounding Mecklenburg County must be integrated at once to achieve student bodies composed of approximately 71 percent white students and 29 percent black students, which reflected the general population of the area. District court judge James McMillan redrew school districts to ensure that no district served an only-white or only-black population. He also ordered the busing of thirteen thousand students to ensure that each school was racially mixed. McMillan's order, particularly his busing plan, was not well received around the country. Many people felt that the courts were now going too far to push school integration.

But when the case, titled *Swan v. Charlotte-Mecklenburg Board of Education*, was appealed to the Supreme Court, the High Court upheld his decision. McMillan's busing plan, wrote Chief Justice Burger, was "reasonable, feasible and workable." For the first time, the Supreme Court had specifically promoted busing as a means of integrating schools that served all-white or all-black neighborhoods or school districts. As a result of the Court's decision, many courts and school boards around the United States implemented busing plans as a strategy for integrating schools.

Many Americans frowned on busing. Parents of school-age children complained that court-ordered busing forced students to attend schools far from their neighborhoods. Suburban school

In 1971 the Supreme Court promoted busing as a means of integrating schools that were racially divided.

boards argued that busing would ruin excellent suburban schools by forcing the schools to enroll academically inferior inner-city students. Some parents of black children even opposed busing on the grounds that it made their children feel like interlopers in previously all-white schools.

Perhaps because of this public backlash against busing, the Supreme Court, in two later cases involving Richmond, Virginia, and Detroit, Michigan, put limits on the use of busing as a method of integrating schools. The Court had approved the busing of students within school districts; but in the Richmond and Detroit cases, the Court ruled that lower courts cannot compel school boards to bus students from one school district to another to achieve integration. Thus, as more and more white families abandoned the inner cities during the 1970s and 1980s, most inner-city schools, in both the North and South, became virtually all-black institutions.

Quality Education?

The final question concerning the legacy of *Brown v. Board of Education* concerns the quality of education available for African American students. One of the key reasons that the NAACP had fought school segregation so vigorously was the belief that the South's Jim Crow schools offered black children an inferior education. If school segregation were outlawed, argued the NAACP, black students would be able to attend higher-quality schools. But did the Supreme Court's call for an end to segregation in public schools actually result in better educational opportunities for black children?

In *The Burden of Brown: Thirty Years of School Desegregation*, published thirty years after the Supreme Court's school desegregation decision, historian Raymond Wolters argues that court-ordered school desegregation has failed. Wolters carefully studied the five school districts that were involved in the *Brown v. Board of Education* and *Bolling v. Sharpe* cases and "found much that is discouraging about what has happened to public education and to the Constitution." In those districts, according to Wolters, "education has suffered grievously." Academic standards and performance have declined, and behavioral problems among students have become more common. Moreover, racial tensions in the schools and in their surrounding neighborhoods have escalated. He concludes his study by making the following charge: "Despite the benefits that blacks and the nation have gained from the prohibition of official segregation, I believe it must be conceded that integration has been a failure in four of the five *Brown* districts."

But Wolters's study concerns only five school districts. What has happened around the nation? Are black students better off today than they were when they attended Jim Crow schools?

Jonathan Kozol, one of the foremost critics of American education, thinks not. In his 1991 book, *Savage Inequalities: Children in America's Schools,* Kozol examines several schools that serve largely black and Latino populations, and he is gravely disheartened by what he sees. He judges the schools in his study to be grossly inferior to suburban schools that serve mostly white children. "What seems unmistakable, but, oddly enough, is rarely

---

In the decades that followed Brown v. Board of Education *critics argued that education for black students had not significantly improved.*

said in public settings nowadays," states Kozol, "is that the nation, for all practice and intent, has turned its back upon the moral implications, if not the ramifications, of the *Brown* decision." Kozol points out, for example, that the school board of Princeton, New Jersey, where the student population in public schools is mainly white, spent $7,725 per student during the 1988-1989 school year. That same year in Camden, New Jersey, where the school population is virtually all nonwhite, only $3,538 was spent to educate each public school pupil. Similar statistics are repeated across the United States. According to Kozol, many of today's schools with a majority of African American students are not much better than the Jim Crow schools of the South before 1954.

Kozol's argument cannot be easily dismissed. In too many of America's urban schools with nonwhite student populations, classrooms are overcrowded, buildings are in disrepair, and educational tools such as computers and laboratory equipment are in short supply. Nonetheless, few American educators would argue that schooling for African American students has not improved since the days of segregated schools. Most of today's African American students are far better educated than their parents and grandparents. The percentage of African American youths who have completed high school and gone on to college has greatly increased. As a result, professions in the United States that were once virtually closed to citizens of color have now opened their doors to African Americans with high school and college diplomas in hand.

Sadly, offering quality education to African American children has remained a national problem. Perhaps the *Brown v. Board of Education* ruling could not on its own completely solve such a serious and widespread problem; perhaps Americans expected too much of a written opinion handed down by nine middle-aged men. Nonetheless, few would maintain that the words of Chief Justice Earl Warren left America unchanged.

Timeline

1865

The Thirteenth Amendment is ratified, freeing all slaves in the United States.

1868

The Fourteenth Amendment is ratified, guaranteeing all citizens equal protection of the law.

1870

The Fifteenth Amendment is passed, guaranteeing all male citizens the right to vote.

1875

Congress passes the Civil Rights Act of 1875, which attempts to outlaw discrimination in hotels, theaters, and other public places.

1896

The Supreme Court's decision in *Plessy v. Ferguson* establishes the "separate but equal" doctrine.

1899

In *Cumming v. Richmond County*, the Supreme Court rules that the courts cannot interfere with local school boards.

1908

In the *Berea College v. Kentucky* decision, the Supreme Court forces integrated Berea College to segregate its classes.

1927

In *Gong Lum v. Rice*, the Supreme Court gives Mississippi the right to designate children as "white" or "colored" for the purpose of assigning them to public schools.

1936

A U.S. appeals court's decision in *Murray v. Maryland* desegregates the University of Maryland School of Law.

1938

In *Gaines v. Canada*, the Supreme Court desegregates the University of Missouri School of Law.

1949

The *Briggs v. Elliott* lawsuit is filed in South Carolina.

1950

The NAACP gains victories in the *McLaurin v. Oklahoma State Regents for Higher Education* and *Sweatt v. Painter* lawsuits.

1951

The *Brown v. Board of Education* lawsuit is filed in Topeka, Kansas.

Two school segregation lawsuits, *Belton v. Gebhart* and *Bulah v. Gebhart*, are filed in Delaware.

The *Davis v. County School Board of Prince Edward County* lawsuit is filed in Virginia.

December 9–11, 1952

The Supreme Court hears the first round of oral arguments in *Brown v. Board of Education* appeals.

December 7–9, 1953

The Supreme Court hears rearguments in the *Brown v. Board of Education* case.

May 17, 1954

The Supreme Court issues its opinion in *Brown v. Board of Education*, outlawing segregation in America's public schools.

May 31, 1955

In *Brown v. Board of Education II*, the Supreme Court urges the nation's school boards to desegregate "with all deliberate speed."

1956–1957

The Montgomery bus boycott forces the city of Montgomery, Alabama, to end segregated seating aboard municipal buses.

September 1957

A crisis develops in Little Rock, Arkansas, when nine black students integrate Central High School.

September 1962

James Meredith becomes the first black student to attend the University of Mississippi.

1964

President Lyndon Johnson signs into law the Civil Rights Act of 1964, outlawing segregation in hotels, restaurants, stadiums, and other public places.

1965

President Johnson signs into law the Voting Rights Acts, guaranteeing all U.S. citizens the right to vote.

For Further Reading

Carson Clayborne et al., eds., *The Eyes on the Prize Civil Rights Reader: Documents, Speeches, and Firsthand Accounts from the Black Freedom Struggle, 1954–1990*. New York: Penguin Books, 1991. Offers a history of the Civil Rights movement and provides excerpts from key civil rights documents.

Martin Luther King Jr., *I Have a Dream: Writing and Speeches That Changed the World*. San Francisco: HarperSanFrancisco, 1992. A collection of King's major speeches and writings.

Harvard Sitkoff, *The Struggle for Black Equality, 1954–1980*. New York: Hill and Wang, 1981. An excellent overview of the Civil Rights movement that begins with the Supreme Court's decision in *Brown v. Board of Education*.

Sanford Wexler, *The Civil Rights Movement: An Eyewitness History*. New York: Facts On File, 1993. An illustrated history of the struggle for racial equality in the United States, commencing with the Civil War and extending through the 1960s. Each chapter contains a chronicle of events and eyewitness testimony.

Elder Witt, ed., *The Supreme Court and Its Work*. Washington, DC: Congressional Quarterly, 1981. Offers an excellent overview of the workings of the Supreme Court, its cases, and its justices.

C. Van Woodward, *The Strange Career of Jim Crow*. New York: Oxford University Press, 1966. A history of the Jim Crow era in American history from its beginnings after the Civil War through its demise during the Civil Rights movement.

Works Consulted

Albert P. Blaustein and Robert L. Zangrando, eds., *Civil Rights and the Negro: A Documentary History*. New York: Trident Press, 1968. A collection of key documents pertaining to the struggle for equal rights for black Americans.

John Egerton, *Speak Now Against the Day: The Generation Before the Civil Rights Movement in the South*. New York: Alfred A. Knopf, 1995. The story of those who fought for racial equality during the decades preceding the *Brown v. Board of Education* case.

Eric Foner and John A. Garraty, eds., *The Reader's Companion to American History*. Boston: Houghton Mifflin, 1991. A single-volume encyclopedia of American history.

David Halberstam, *The Fifties*. New York: Villard Books, 1993. A comprehensive history of the United States during the 1950s.

Richard Kluger, *Simple Justice: The History of Brown v. Board of Education and Black America's Struggle for Equality*. New York: Alfred A. Knopf, 1976. A detailed study of the *Brown v. Board of Education* case.

Jonathan Kozol, *Savage Inequalities: Children in America's Schools*. New York: HarperPerennial, 1991. An analysis of the problems of urban schools during the 1990s.

Raymond Wolters, *The Burden of Brown: Thirty Years of School Desegregation*. Knoxville: University of Tennessee Press, 1984. An analysis of the school districts covered in the *Brown v. Board of Education* case thirty years after the Supreme Court's desegregation decision.

Bob Woodward and Scott Armstrong, *The Brethren: Inside the Supreme Court*. New York: Simon and Schuster, 1979. A history of the Supreme Court during the Earl Warren years.

Index

106

Picture Credits

Cover photo: UPI/Corbis-Bettmann

Archive Photos, 30, 44, 99

Corbis-Bettmann, 28

Library of Congress, 8, 17, 19, 23, 24, 26, 32, 34, 37, 42, 49, 50, 60, 71, 79, 81, 87, 91

North Wind Picture Archives, 13

Schomburg Center for Research in Black Culture, 55, 58, 94

Stock Montage, Inc., 14, 69, 74

UPI/Corbis-Bettmann, 40, 48, 64, 66, 76, 83, 84, 88, 97

About the Author

James Tackach is the author of young adult biographies of Roy Campanella, Henry Aaron, and James Baldwin. He has also authored *Historic Homes of America*, *Great American Hotels*, and *Fields of Summer: America's Great Ballparks and the Players Who Triumphed in Them*. His articles have appeared in the *New York Times*, the *Providence Journal*, *America's Civil War*, and a variety of academic publications. He teaches American literature at Roger Williams University, Bristol, Rhode Island, and lives in Narragansett, Rhode Island.